The Art of
Man-Fishing

The Art of
Man-Fishing

Thomas Boston

Sovereign Grace Publishers, Inc.
P.O. Box 4998
Lafayette, IN 47903

Printed In the United States of America
By Lightning Source, Inc.

THE ART OF MAN-FISHING.

INTRODUCTION

Lord, who has believed our report? and to whom is the arm of the Lord revealed? This day seems to be a day of darkness and gloominess; the glory is departed even to the threshold of the temple. We may call the faithful preachers no more Naomi, but Marah, for the Lord deals bitterly with them. The Lord has forsaken them in a great measure, as to success attending their labors. They toil all the night; but little or nothing is caught: few or none can they find to come into the net. So that Jeremiah's lament may be theirs, 13:17, *"If you will not hear it, my soul shall weep in secret places for your pride; and my eye shall weep sore, and run down with tears."*

And now dear reader, are you one of those who are called out to preach the everlasting gospel, and is it your endeavor and your desire to be a fisher of men? But, alas! you come in with complaints to the Lord, that you have toiled in some measure, but caught nothing, for all that you know, as to the conversion of any one soul. And do you ask what may be the cause of this, why your preaching does so little good? No doubt you feel part of the blame lies in yourself, and a great part of it too. But who can give help in this case but the Lord Himself? and how can you expect it from Him except by prayer, and faith in the promises, and by consulting His word where you may, by His Spirit shining on your heart, learn how to carry the gospel? Does your heart cry out after Christ, then, when you read that sweet promise of Christ, Matt. 4:19, *Follow me, and I will make you fishers of men,* directed to those that would follow him? Then study these words, and let this be your prayer: "O let Thy light and Thy truth shine forth, that they may be guides to me in this matter; and let the meditations of my heart be according to Thy mind, and directed by Thy unerring Spirit. Grant light and full life, O Lord my God!"

FOLLOW ME, AND I WILL MAKE YOU FISHERS OF MEN.

In these words there are two things to be considered.

1. There is a duty, Follow me. In this consider,

(1) The object, me, even the Lord Jesus Christ, the chief fisher of men, who was sent by the Father to gather in the lost sheep of the house of Israel, who was and is the infinitely-wise God, and so knew the best way to catch men, and can instruct men how to be fishers of others.

(2) The act, Follow (Gr. come after) me: Leave your employment, and come after Me. This means a Christian's employment should be left behind when he has Christ's call to do His bidding.

2. There is a promise annexed to the duty. In it we may consider,

(I) The benefit promised; that is, to be made fishers of men; which is not only an investing of them with authority, and a calling of them to the office, but also a promise of the success they should have, that fishing of men should be their employment, and they should not be employed in vain, but following Christ, they should indeed catch men by the gospel.

(2) The fountain-cause of this, I, I will make you; none other can make you fishers of men but Christ.

In opening the verse we shall observe that the way to become a fisher of men is found in the duty, Follow me. And this we take up second in Division II. But then, it must be observed that following Christ is all that can be done in becoming a fisher of men, for the latter part of the verse shows us that the Christian's actual becoming a fisher of men is not something that he himself does, but it is something that Christ does according to the promise, And I will make you fishers of men. To stir up the reader to this duty, we consider first the motive found in the promise itself. This we take up in Division I.

DIVISION I

Observe, then, that it is the Lord Jesus Christ that makes men fishers of men. Here I shall show, First, Why unconverted men are compared to fish in the water; and Secondly, In what way Christ makes men fishers of men.

First, Why are unconverted men compared to fish in the water? Among other reasons, they are so, —

1. Because as the water is the natural element of fish, so sin is the proper and natural element for an unconverted soul. Take the fish out of the water, it cannot live; and take from a natural man his idols, he is ready to say with Micah, You have taken away my gods, and what do I have left? The rich young man could not be persuaded to lay aside the world and seek treasure in heaven by following Christ. It is in sin that the only delight of natural men is; but they do not have any more delight in holiness than a fish has in the dry land, or a sow in a palace. Oh the woeful case of the natural man!

2. The fish in a sunny day are seen to play in the water. So the unregenerate, whatever grief they may seem to have upon their spirits when a storm arises, either by outward troubles or by conscience-gnawing convictions within, yet when these are over and they are prosperous, they play themselves in the way of sin and take their pleasure in it, not considering what it may cost them at the last. Oh, how prosperity in the world ruins many a soul! The prosperity of fools shall destroy them.

3. As the fish greedily look after and snatch at the bait, ignoring the hook; even so natural men drink in sin greedily, as the ox drinks in the water. They look on sin as a sweet tidbit; and it is to them sweet in the mouth, though bitter in the belly. They play with it, as the fish with the

bait; but, alas, when they take the serpent in their bosom, they do not know the sting (Prov. 9:17,18). The devil knows well how to dress his hooks; but, alas, by nature men do not know how to discern them. Pity then, the wicked of the world, that you see greedily satisfying their lusts. Alas! they are poor blinded souls; they see the bait, but not the hook. And therefore it is as if that they are seen dancing about the mouth of the pit; they rush on to sin as a horse to the battle, not knowing the hazard. Pity the poor drunkard, the swearer, and the unclean person that is wallowing in his sin! And the Lord also, that when you were playing with the bait and paying as little attention to the hook as others, God opened your eyes and let you see your madness and danger, so that you might flee from it. And be careful now that you snatch at none of the devil's baits, lest he catch you with his hook: because though you may be restored again by grace, yet it shall not be without a wound; as the fish sometimes slip the hook, but go away wounded, such a wound would be sad to you, and take long in healing.

4. As fish in the water love deep places and wells, and are most frequently found there; so wicked men have a great love to carnal security, and have no will to strive against the stream. Fish love deep places best, where there is least noise. O how careful are natural men to keep all quiet, that there may be nothing to disturb them in their rest in sin! They love to be secure, and that is their destruction. O my soul, beware of carnal security, of being secure, though plunged over head and ears in sin.

5. As fish are unprofitable as long as they are in the water, so are wicked men in their natural estate. They can do nothing that is really good: they are unprofitable to themselves, and unprofitable to others. What good they do to others, is more by accident that good in itself (Rom. 3:12). How much are they mistaken, then, who think the wicked of the world are the most useful in the place where they live! They may indeed be useful for carrying on designs for Satan's interest or their own vain glory; but really they cannot lay out themselves for God.

Secondly, in what way does Christ make men fishers of men?

In answer to this question, consider spiritual fishing two ways. I. As to the success of it; and II. As to the office and work itself,

I. He makes them fishers as to success; that is, He makes them catch men to Himself by the power of His spirit accompanying the word they preach, 1 Cor. 1:18, *The preaching of the cross — to us which are saved, it is the power of God.* I Thess. 1:5, *Our gospel came not unto you in word only, but also in power, and in the Holy Spirit, and in much assurance.* It is He that brings sinners into the net which ministers spread; and if He is not with them to drive the fish into the net, they may toil all the night, and all day too, and catch nothing.

1. then see that all of a man's gifts will not bring him success. A man

may preach as an angel, and yet be useless. If Christ withdraws His presence, all will be to no purpose.

2. Why should anyone, on the one hand, be lifted up when he preaches a good and solid discourse, in which his gifts appear, and he gets the applause of men? He may do all this, and yet not be a fisher of men. On the other hand, why should someone be discouraged because his gifts are so small, and he is but as a child in comparison to others? Why, if Christ will, he can make him a fisher of men, as well as the most learned rabbi. *Out of the mouths of babes and sucklings hast thou ordained strength.* (Ps. 8:2). Have you not observed how God took a man very weak in gifts and made him more successful than others that were far beyond him? Has not God put this treasure in earthen vessels, that the power might be seen to be of him? Lift up yourself then, Christ can make you a fisher of men, however weak you are. Follow Him.

3. Be concerned then, in the first place, for the presence of God, and for His power that will make a change among people (Ps. 110:3). O, power and life from God is sweet. Seek it for yourself and seek it for your hearers. Acknowledge your own weakness and uselessness without it, and so cry continually for it, that the Lord may drive the fish into the net, when you are spreading it out. Have an eye to this power, when you are preaching; and do not think you can convert men by the force of reason. If you do, you will be fooled.

4. What an honorable thing it is to be fishers of men! How great an honor you should think it is, to be a catcher of souls! We are workers together with God, says the apostle. If God has ever honored you so, O that you knew it, that you might bless His holy name.

5. Then don't you see here what the reason is that you toil so long, and catch nothing? The power does not come along with it. Men are like Samuel, who when God was calling him, thought it had been Eli. So many times when you speak they do not hear God's voice, but yours; and therefore the word goes out as it comes in.

6. Then, also, do not despair of the conversion of any, no matter how bad they are. For it is the power of the Spirit that drives any person into the net; and this cannot be resisted. Mockers of religion, yes, blasphemers may be brought into the net; and many times the wind of God's Spirit in the word lays those who are as tall in sin as cedars down upon the ground, when those who seem to be as low shrubs in comparison to them, stand fast upon their root. Publicans and harlots shall enter the kingdom of heaven before self-righteous Pharisees.

7. What do you think of that doctrine that lays aside this power of the Spirit, and makes moral suasion all that is necessary to fishing for men? You must have it, as attributing too much to the preacher and too much to corrupt nature in taking away its natural impotency to good. And it is

both against the work of God's Spirit and contrary to experience. To me it is a sign of the rottenness of the heart that embraces it. Alas, that it should be held by any among us, where so much of the Spirit's power has been felt!

II. Christians are fishers by office; they are those who carry the gospel and preach it; they are catchers of the souls of men, sent to open the eyes of the blind, and to turn them from darkness to light, and from the power of Satan unto God. Those who carry the gospel are fishers, and their work and that of fishers agree in several things.

1. The purpose and work of fishers is to catch fish. This is the work that preachers of the gospel have taken in hand, even to endeavor to bring souls to Christ. Their purpose in their work should be the same.

2. Their work is hard work; they are exposed to much cold in the water. So is the Christian's work.

3. A storm that will frighten others, they will go out in, that they may not lose their fish. Preachers of the gospel should do the same thing.

4. Fishers catch fish with a net. Preachers also have a net to catch souls with. This is the everlasting gospel, the word of peace and reconciliation, with which sinners are caught. It is compared to a net with which fishers catch fish,

(1) Because it is spread out, ready to catch all who will come into it, *Ho, every one who thirsts, come to the waters; and he who has no money, come buy, and eat; yes, come, buy wine and milk, without money, and without price* (Isa. 55:1). God excludes none from the benefits of the gospel who do not exclude themselves; it is free to all.

(2) Because as fish are taken unexpectedly by the net, so are sinners by the gospel. Zaccheus was little thinking on salvation from Christ when he went up into the tree. Paul was not thinking on a sweet meeting with Christ, whom he persecuted, when he was going post-haste on the devil's errand; but the man was caught unexpectedly.

(3) As fish sometimes come near and touch the net, and yet draw back; so many souls are somewhat affected at the hearing of the gospel, and yet remain in the gall of bitterness and the bond of iniquity. Herod heard John the Baptist gladly in this way, but yet the poor man was not caught. Do not wonder then, that you see some affected at the time of preaching and yet when they are away again all is worn off.

(4) Some fish that have not been caught securely enough by the net struggle and get out again. So some souls have their convictions, and may seem to be taken; but yet, alas! they stifle all their convictions, and are as the early morning dew that soon passes away. Therefore, whenever you are taken up with those whose consciences are worked up, by all means take

care to understand whether the soul is content to take Christ on his own terms or not.

(5) All that are taken in the net do make some struggling to get free. Even so every one whom the Lord deals with by His Word and Spirit, make some kind of resistance before they are thoroughly caught.

And wouldn't you have been content to have been out of the net? Oh, the wickedness of the heart of man by nature! It is contrary and an enemy to all that may be for its own eternal welfare. There is indeed a power in our will to resist, yes, and it is such a power as cannot but be exercised by the will of man, which can do nothing but resist, until the overcoming power of God, that victorious grace come and make the unwilling heart willing (Phil. 2:13).

(6) Yet this struggling will not do with those that the net has securely enough. So neither will the resistance do that is made by an elect soul, whom God intends to catch. *All that the Father has given me, shall come to me* (John 6:37). Indeed, God does not convert men to Himself against their will; He does not force the soul to receive Christ. But He conquers the will, and it becomes obedient. He who was unwilling before, is then O the power of grace! When God speaks, then men shall hear. It is then that the dead hear the voice of the Son of Man, and that those who hear live.

(7) In a net are many meshes in which the fish are caught. Such are the invitations made to sinners in the gospel, the sweet promises made to those who will come to Christ; these are the meshes in which the soul is caught. This then is gospel preaching, to spread out the net of the gospel, so that there are so many meshes of various invitations and promises to which, if the fish do come, they are caught.

(8) But yet, so that the net will not be lifted up with the water and not fit for taking fish — the fish slight it, and pass under it — there are some pieces of lead put to it, to hold it down in the water, that it may be before them as they come. In the same way invitations and promises of the gospel will not be slighted, there some legal terrors and law-threatenings must be used to drive the fish into the net. You see then that both law and gospel are to be preached, the law as a pendicle of the gospel-net, which makes it effective; the law being a schoolmaster to bring us to Christ.

(9) The meshes must not be too far apart, or else the fish run through. In the same way your doctrine must not be general, without particular application, or you will not be a fisher of men. Men may indeed be the better pleased, when you preach doctrine in such a way that wicked men may run out-through and in-through it, than when you make it so that it takes hold of them. But be not a servant of men!

(10) But the meshes must not be too neat and fine, and made close, lest they hold out the fish. So have a care not to strive to make any fine and

exact message by reason which your hearers cannot understand.

5. Fishers notice what places they should throw their nets, and where they may expect fish. So you too notice where you may catch souls. There are two pools in which the net should be set.

(1) In the public meetings. There it was that Lydia's heart was opened. The pool of worship services sometimes is made to be healing water to souls pining away in their iniquity.

(2) In private conversations.

6. Lastly, as fishers may toil long and yet catch nothing, but they do not lay aside their work; so preachers may preach long and yet not catch any soul (Isa. 49:4, and 53:1). It is appropriate to lie low under God's hand and to inquire into the causes of His withdrawing of His presence but yet to continue to hold on in duty until He is pleased to set you aside. Christ may come and teach you to let down the net at the right side of the ship, so that you may still become a fisher of men. Trust God and you will yet praise Him for the help of His countenance and perhaps for some souls that you may yet be honored to catch.

DIVISION II

The main question that should now be resolved is, How may I come by this art? what path shall I take to be a fisher of men? and, how may I arrange and set the net, that it may bring in souls to God? This, the great Master sets down in the first part of the verse.

Observe, then, that the way to be a fisher of men is to follow Christ. What is it to follow the Lord?

Here two things are to be considered.

First, what following Christ presupposes and implies.

Secondly, in what way Christ is to be followed.

First, what following Christ presupposes and implies.

I. It presupposes life. A dead man cannot follow any person; a dead preacher cannot follow Christ. There must be a principle of life, spiritual life in him, or else he is nothing. Therefore have I said and maintained, that a man cannot be a minister speaking for God though he may be speaking for the church without grace in his heart. This is to follow Christ spiritually; and therefore presupposes a spiritual and heavenly principle. Tell me then, what state you are in? Has Christ breathed on your dead and dry bones? or are you still lacking spiritual life and rotting away in your iniquity? What can you say to this?

1. A man who has the Spirit has life (Rom. 8:2,9). Do you think you have the Spirit: and so have life? You may conclude that you have the Spirit from these following grounds.

(1) There is light that at one time you did not have. *The Comforter — shall teach you all things, and bring all things to your remembrance*

whatsoever I have said to you (John 14:26). Once you were blind, but now you see, though you only see men as trees. Once you were darkness, but now light (though weak) in the Lord. This light makes you see,

[1] Your former darkness, the sad and miserable state that you were once in, ignorant of God, Christ, and religion, except, perhaps, going to the church, and keeping from swearing, and so forth. But that was because you were restrained from them, from a child.

[2] It lets you see your heart-sins, imperfections, and shortcomings even in the best of performance; so that God might damn me for them. The hypocrites say, *Why have we fasted, and you do see not* (Isa. 58:3)?

[3] It makes you see that Christ is precious (1 Pet. 2:7), altogether lovely, the chief among ten thousand, preferable to all the world; for whom, if your heart does not deceive you, you would undergo the loss of that which you most esteem in the world. *"Whom do I have in heaven but You? and there is none on earth that I desire besides You."* For indeed, *"My heart and flesh faints and fails; but You are the strength of my heart, O Lord"* (Psa. 78: 25–26).

[4] It lets you see your need of Him; so that nothing else but Christ, you are persuaded, can help you. When you have done what you can, you are only an unprofitable servant. If you should do a thousand times more than you do, you would count all but loss and dung for the excellency of the knowledge of Jesus Christ your Lord.

[5] The knowledge that you have of Christ, makes you trust in Him in some measure (Psa. 9:10). You find Him a present help in the time of trouble; and therefore cast your burden upon Him.

(2) You feel help in your performance from the Spirit. Though you do not know what you should pray for, the Spirit helps your infirmities (Rom. 8:26).

2. He who has sense and feeling has life (Eph. 4:18-19). His sins are a burden to him (Matt. 11:28). The body of sin and death makes him groan, and long to be rid of it (Rom. 7:24).

3. He in whom there is the warmth of Christ has life. There is a threefold flame, though weak, in his heart:

(1) A flame of love to Christ (Rom. 5:5). The soul loves Him above all. He has a love to His truths (Psa. 119:19). He may find His word sweeter than honey from the comb (Psa. 19:10). It comforts and supports him. He cannot but love it; it stirs him up, and quickens his soul. He loves His commands, though they strike against his corruptions (Rom. 7:22). The promises are as sweet cordials to a fainting soul, as life from the dead to one trodden under foot by the apprehensions of wrath, or the prevailing of corruption. His threatenings are most just, and his soul heartily approves them. If any man love not the Lord Jesus, let him be anathema,

maranatha. The least part of truth, that God makes known to him, he loves; and, by grace, would endeavor to adhere to. He loves those in whom the image of God appears; though otherwise poor and contemptible, his heart warms towards them (1 John 3:14). He loves His work, and is glad when it thrives (Rom. 1:8).

(2) A flame of holy desires (Matt. 5:6).

[1] After the righteousness of Christ. The soul earnestly desires to be stript naked of his own righteousness, which is as rags, and to be clothed and adorned with the robe of His righteousness. The soul is satisfied, and acquiesces in justification by an imputed righteousness.

[2]After communion with Him (Psa. 42:1). When he wants it, the soul though sometimes careless, yet, at other times, cries out, O that I knew where I might find Him! He has found much sweetness, in communion with God, especially at the sacrament of the Lord's supper, in prayer and meditation, hearing the Word faithfully and seriously preached. Sometimes he longs for the day when his preparation shall be past, and he shall have entered heir to the inheritance incorruptible, undefiled, and that fades not away; to be through with this evil world; to be dissolved and to be with Christ, which is best of all.

(3) Zeal for God, which vents itself. First, by endeavoring to be active for God. Secondly, in indignation against sin in oneself and others. When you have been overcome by a temptation, are you content to write down a sentence of judgement against yourself and so to justify the Lord in His just proceedings against you? But also, *Lord, do I not hate those that hate You? Am I not grieved with those that rise up against You? The reproaches cast on You, have fallen on me* (Psa. 69:9). Is the heart grieved when it sees transgressors that do not keep God's law? Thirdly, in grieving for those things that one cannot prevent. How heavy are the sins of this land! There is such laxness of many in joining together with the wicked. There is the unfaithfulness of some who profess to know Christ, the lack of zeal for God in failing to search for the accursed thing in our camp. God's wrath is going out violently against us.

4. Growth and motion is an evidence of life (Psalm 92:12-14). Do you move forward towards heaven, with affections going out after Christ, and endeavor to make progress in a Christian walk? Do you discern a growth of the following graces in you?

(1) Of knowledge and acquaintance with Christ (1 Pet 3:18). You should be more acquainted with Christ and His ways than before. Though you have not taken up Christ and His ways as you ought there has been a definite change.

(2) A growth of love. Love to Christ grows each month more lively and vigorous than before, and the soul more affected with His absence from worship than ever.

(3) Of faith. There has been an increase in faith in God. As one has more experience of His goodness and knowledge of His name, he can cast his burden on the Lord better than before. But it is easy swimming when the head is held up. *I believe, Lord, help mine unbelief.*

(4) Of watchfulness. Have you felt the sad effects of unwatchfulness over your heart in times past? Now is your soul habitually more watchful than before?

(5) Of contempt of the world. This should always be on the increase with you.

II. Following Christ implies a knowledge of the way that Christ took. No man can follow the example of another unless he knows what way he lived. So neither can any man follow Christ with respect to the catching of men, unless he knows Christ's way of catching souls, at least, as far as it may be followed by us. Acquaint yourself, then, with the history of the gospel in which this appears, and take special notice of these things, so that you may follow Christ. What a sad situation it is for those who are not acquainted with this!

III. It supposes sense of weakness, and the need of a guide. A man who knows a way, and can do well enough without a guide, does not need to follow another. And surely the lack of knowing the way is the reason why many run ahead of Christ, and go farther than His example ever called them. Others take a way altogether different from Christ's way, one which is the product of their own conceited hearts and airy heads. But you acknowledge yourself to be like a child in these matters, that cannot go unless it be led; like a stranger in a desert who cannot keep on the right path without a guide. Acknowledge and be affected by your own weakness and emptiness. And to do this reflect seriously (1) On that word, *Who is sufficient for these things* (2 Cor. 2:16)? No man is of himself sufficient; even the greatest of men come short of sufficiency. How, then, should you act, who are so far below these men, just as shrubs are below the tall cedars; and yet they cannot teach it of themselves. (2) Consider the weight of the work, especially, of preaching. It is what matters to souls. By the foolishness of preaching it pleases the Lord to save those who believe. It may seal the salvation of some, and the damnation of others. To speak in the Spirit, in the power and demonstration of Him, is no easy matter. (3) Reflect on what you are when God is pleased to desert you; how you then tug and row, but it will not do, either in studying or speaking (including delivering sermons). Beware of taking your burden on your own soul, but cast it on the Lord. (4) Consider how little you know of God. When you are at your best and when you are in your meridian, yet how low you are! and how far short you come from what you should be. (5) Lastly, consider that though you had gifts like an angel, yet you could not convert a soul unless Christ was with you to do the work. Therefore acknowledge yourself to be a weak creature, insufficient for the work; and do not go out in your own strength, but in the name of the Lord. And so although you are only as a youth, you may be used to throw down the great Goliaths that defy the armies of the living God.

IV. It implies a renouncing of our own wisdom. That wisdom must not be the guide that we must follow (Matt. 16:24). Paul would not preach with the wisdom of words (1 Cor. 1:17); he did not follow the rules of human wisdom. Therefore, seek the wisdom that is from above; seek to speak the words of the living God, and not your own. But hear and follow the rules of the wisdom that is from above: for the wisdom of the world is foolishness with God; that which is in high esteem among men, is nothing in the sight of God. The wisdom that is from above will tell you that you must be denied your credit and reputation (Matt. 16:24; Luke 14:26). It will tell you, Let them call you what they will, that you must *cry aloud, and spare not; lift up your voice like a trumpet* (Isa. 58:1). It will tell you that *God has appointed the bounds of men's habitation* (Acts 17:26). It will tell you that *not many wise, not many mighty, not many noble, are called* (1 Cor. 1:20). *Whether they will hear, or whether they will forbear, you shall speak God's words to them* (Ezek. 2:7). It will show you rules quite contrary to those of human wisdom. Consider then what human wisdom says, and what the wisdom from above says.

HUMAN WISDOM.

Your body is weak, spare it, and do not let it get weary; it cannot stand toil, labor, and weariness; spare thyself then.

Labor to get neat and fine expressions; for these do very much commend themselves to the well educated; and without these they ignore you.

SPIRITUAL WISDOM.

Your body is God's as well as your spirit; do not spare it in glorifying God (1 Cor. 6:20). *"In weariness and painfulness"* (2 Cor. 11:27). *"He gives power to the faint, and to those that have no might He increases strength"* (Isa 40:29).

Christ sent you to *"preach the gospel not with wisdom of words"* (1 Cor. 1:17). Do not go to them with *"excellency of speech, or of wisdom"* (1 Cor. 2:1). Do not let your speech be with *"the enticing words of man's wisdom"* (1 Cor. 2:4).

Endeavor to speak calmly. And do not go into the particular sins of the land or the people to whom thou speak.

"Cry aloud, and spare not, lift up your voice like a trumpet: show my people their sins" (Isa. 58:1). *"Open rebuke is better than secret love"* (Prov. 27:5). *"Study to show yourself approved to God, rightly dividing the word of truth"* (2 Tim. 2:15).

If you will not speak gently they will be irritated against you, and may create trouble; and what a foolish thing it would be for you to speak boldly to such a generation as this, whose very looks are terrible?

"He who rebukes a man, afterwards shall find more favor than he who flatters with the tongue" (Prov. 28:23). *"Fear them not, neither be afraid at their looks, though they are a rebellious house. I have made your face strong against their faces.* (Ezek. 3:8-9).

It is a dangerous way to speak freely and come down to particulars: there may be more hazard in it than you are aware of.

"He who walks uprightly, walks surely" (Prov. 10:9). *"Whoso walks uprightly shall be saved"* (Prov. 28:18).

Do you want to be looked on as a fool, as a monster; do you want to be called a blow-hard; and so lose your reputation. You had better preserve that. Men will hate and reject you; and why should you expose yourself to these things?

"You must become a fool, that you may be wise" (1 Cor. 3:18). *"We are made a spectacle to the world"* (1 Cor. 4:9). *"The servant is not greater than his lord"* (John 5:20; cf. 10:20). *"He has a devil, and is crazy; why do you listen to him?"* If you will be Christ's disciple, *"you must deny yourself"* (Matt. 16:24).

"If the world hate you, you know it hated me before it hated you" says our Lord (John 15:18).

Great people especially will be offended at you, if you do not speak nicely to them. And if you are looked down upon by great people, who are wise and powerful, then how will you feel?

Our people are immature Christians and they would not like to have particular sins told to them, and especially old sores to be ripped up. They cannot stand that teaching. Different doctrines would take better. Hold off on such things; for it may well hurt them and will do them no good.

If you will speak such things, yet prudence requires that you speak of them very cautiously. Though conscience says you must, yet speak them in a somewhat disguised way, so that you may not offend them and especially those who are just coming in yet, and do not fill them with unsubstantiated truths which you may get occasion afterwards.

Be gentle until you are settled in a church. If you will not do so, you may look forward to toiling up and down; for churches will be afraid of you, and will not call you, and, if you are a pastor, how will you live? And so such

"Accept no man's person, neither give flattering titles to man: for, in so doing, your Maker will soon take you away" (Job 32:21-22). *"Few of the rulers believe on Christ"* (John 7:48). *"Not many wise men after the flesh, not many mighty, not many noble are called"* (1 Cor. 1:26). *"Speak God's word to kings, and be not ashamed"* (Psa. 46).

"You shall speak my words to them, whether they will hear or whether they will shun it, for they are most rebellious" (Ezek. 2:7). *"Give them warning from Me. If you do not do it they shall die in their sins, but their blood will I require at your hand"* (Ezek. 3:17-18). *"What the Lord says to you, speak that"* (1 Kings 22:14).

"Cry aloud, and do not spare" (Isa. 58:1). *"Cursed is he who does the work of the Lord deceitfully"* (Jer. 48:10). Peter, at the first, told the Jews that were just barely coming to hear, *"Him (Christ) you have taken, and by wicked hands have crucified and slain"* (Acts 2:23). *"Work while it is called today; the night comes in you can not work"* (John 9:4).

"To have respect of persons is not good; for, for a piece of bread that man will transgress" (Prov. 28:21). *"The will of the Lord be done"* (Acts 21:14). *"God has determined your time, before appointed, and the bounds of your*

a way of preaching will be to your loss, whereas otherwise it might be better with you.

habitation" (Acts 17:26). *"And His counsel shall stand, oppose it who will"* (Isa. 46:10). *"It is God that sets the solitary in families"* (Psalm 68:6). *"If you are faithful, you shall abound with blessings; but if you make haste to be rich, you shall not be innocent"* (Prov. 28:20)

So notice how human wisdom even though it sounds nice and appears to have a good deal of reason, is quite contrary to the wisdom that is from above. It promises well, but its promises are not always performed. It threatens severely, but also its threatenings do not always come to pass. It makes molehills mountains, and mountains molehills; therefore reject the wisdom of the world, for it is foolishness with God. Human advice would make you fear him who can only kill the body, and to cast off the true fear of God. *The fear of man brings a snare; but whoso puts his trust in the Lord shall be safe* (Prov. 29:25). Never go to seek earthly profit by putting your soul in hazard, but *wait on the Lord, and keep His way, and He shall exalt you to inherit the land* (Psalm 37:34); for His way is the safest way, it pure foolishness to follow; but remember, that *the foolishness of God is wiser than men* (1 Cor. 1:27).

V. It supposes, that we must not make men our rule, to follow them any farther than they follow Christ. *Be followers of me,* says the apostle, *as I am of Christ* (1 Cor. 11:1). All men are fallible; the greatest of men had their own spots. Luther's opinion of Christ's corporal presence in the sacrament affords a notable instance of this. Therefore, let no man's authority prevail with you to go off the road at all.

Secondly, In what way is Christ to be followed; what are those things that you must imitate Him in? What was the model that He made, which must be examined, in order to be a fisher of men? What He did by divine power can not be imitated; one is not called to follow Him in converting sinners by his own power or to work miracles for the confirmation of doctrine, etc. But there are some things in which He can be imitated, and must be followed if one would expect to be made a fisher of men.

1. Christ did not take on Himself the work of preaching the gospel without a call. *"For* (says He) *the Spirit of the Lord God is on Me, because the Lord has anointed Me to preach good tidings to the meek, he has sent Me to bind up the broken-hearted, to proclaim liberty to the captives, and the opening of the prison to them that are bound"* (Isa. 61:1). In this He must be followed by those who would be catchers of men. He was sent by the Father to preach the gospel; He did not begin the work without His Father's commission. Men must have a call to this work (Heb. 5:4). They who run unsent, who take on the work without a call from God, cannot

expect to do good to a people (Rom. 10:14, Jer. 23). *I sent them not, therefore they shall not profit this people.*

Do you have a call from God to this work of preaching the gospel? Or will you run unsent? Let those only whom the Lord Jesus Christ has prepared for this work go forth to carry the gospel. And it is to those who have heard His call, *Follow me,* that He has promised to prepare, to be made fishers of men.

II. Christ sought His Father's glory in His work. It was not honor, applause, and credit from men that He sought, but purely the Father's glory. Men who do not seek this, cannot be useful to the church, except by accident. *Whether therefore you eat or drink, or whatever you do, do all to the glory of God. Do not look for popular applause; if you do, you have your reward* (Matt. 6:2), look for no more. And to help you to do all to God's honor, consider,

1. That all you have is given to you by God. What do you have that you have not received? What an unreasonable thing is it then not to use for His glory what He gives you and don't you hate the character of an ungrateful person?

2. Consider that what you have is a talent given to you by your great Master to improve until He comes again. If you improve it for Him, then you shall get your reward. If you will make your own gain by it, you can look forward to nothing but for God to take your talent from you, and command to throw you as an unprofitable and unfaithful servant into complete darkness, where there shall be weeping and gnashing of teeth. God has given some great talents. If they improve them for vain-glory for themselves to gain the popular applause, or the Hosannas of the learned, what a sad meeting will such have at the great day with Christ! What master would put up with that servant to whom he has given money with which to buy a suit of good clothes for his master, if he should take that money and buy with it a suit for himself, which his master should have had? How can it be thought that God will allow one that He has given a talent of gifts to go unpunished, if he shall use it merely to gain a salary or applause to himself with is not respecting the glory of his Master?

3. Consider that the applause of the world is worth nothing. It is hard to get; for readily the applause of the educated is given to those whom the educated despise, and the educated applaud those whom the common people do not care for. And when the applause is obtained, what do you have? − A vain empty puff of wind. They think much of you, you think much of yourself and in the meantime God thinks nothing of You. Remember what Christ said to the Pharisees, *"You are they which justify yourselves before men, but God knows your hearts. For that which is highly esteemed among men, is an abomination in the sight of God"* (Luke 16:15).

4. Consider, that seeking your own glory is a dreadful and hateful thing. (1) You put yourself in the place of God. His glory should be that which you should aim at, but then your own self must be sacrificed too. (2) It is the worst pretense with God that there can be. You pretend to speak of Christ to people; but seeking your own glory, you preach yourself, and not Him. Will Christ sit with such a mocking of Him? (3) It is low false dealing and cruelty to the souls of hearers when a man seeks to please their fancy more than to gain their souls and to get people to approve him more than to get them to approve themselves to God. This is a soul-murdering way, and it is dear-bought applause that is won by the blood of souls.

5. Consider that to do so is a terrible sign of a graceless, Christless, and faithless heart. *How can you believe, that receive honor one of another, and seek not the honor that comes from God only* (John 5:44)? A grain of faith will cure this lightness of the head and heart.

6. Consider your own vileness. What are you except a poor lump of clay with respect to your body, that will soon return to the dust, and be a sweet tid-bit for the worms that you now trample on! Haven't you seen how many times in life, the body is greatly disliked by filthy boils and other diseases with offensive smells, and after death what an ugly appearance it has?

7. Consider, that "He who honors God, God will honor; but he who despises Him, shall be lightly thought of." Have respect to the recompence of reward, as Moses did, and beware of preferring your own to the interest of Christ, lest you be classed among those who seek their own, and not the things of Christ.

8. Lastly, Consider what Christ has done for you. Do not forget His goodness, His undeserved goodness to such a low miserable person as you are. Remember Him from the land of the Hermonites, and from Mizar-hill; and let love to Him predominate in you, and you shall then be helped to sacrifice all to His glory.

III. Christ had the good of souls in His eye. He came to seek and save that which was lost; He came to seek the lost sheep of the house of Israel. So He sent out the apostle to open the eyes of the blind, to turn them from darkness to light, and from the power of Satan to God. Follow Christ in this so that you may be a fisher of men. Let this be your design, to endeavor to recover lost sheep, to get some brands plucked out of the burning, to get some converted and brought in to your Master. Let that be much in your mind and be concerned for that. Consider for this effect,

1. What the design of the gospel is. What is it but this? This is the ultimate task; and if it is not your ultimate concern, it is very lamentable. It is the everlasting gospel that Christ has made manifest, declaring the will of God concerning the salvation of man.

2. For what reason God sent you out. Was it to win a livelihood for yourself? Woe to them that count gain godliness; that will make the gospel

merely subservient to their earthly wants. It would be better to perish from lack than win bread that way. Well then, was it not to the effect you might labor to gain souls to Christ? Yes, it was. Take heed then that you are not likely to go to a place, but forget the errand when you come there, and trifle away the time in vanity and foolishness.

3. The worth of souls. The soul is a precious thing: which this is clear if you consider, (I) Its noble endowments, adorned with understanding, capable to know the highest object; having a will to choose the same; having affections to pursue after it, to love God, hate sin, in a word, to glorify God here, and to enjoy Him here and hereafter. (2) It must live or die forever. It shall either enjoy God through all the ages of eternity, or remain in endless torments for evermore. (3) No worldly gain can counterbalance the loss of it. "What shall it profit a man, if he should gain the whole world, and lose his own soul? or what shall a man give in exchange for his soul?" (4) It cost Christ His precious blood before it could be redeemed. It was necessary for Him to bear the Father's wrath, so that the elect should have borne through all eternity; and no less would redeem it. Consequently, the redemption of the soul is precious indeed. (5) Christ courts the soul. He stands at the door and knocks, to get in. The devil courts it with his baits and allurements. Will you be unconcerned for the good of that which is so much courted by Christ and the devil both? Be ashamed to stand as an unconcerned spectator, lest you show yourself to be none of the Bridegroom's friends!

4. The hazard that souls are in. Alas, the most part are going on in the highway to destruction, and they are doing it blind-folded. Endeavor then to draw off the veil. They are as sticks in the fire: will you then be so cruel as not as to be concerned to pluck them out? If so, you shalt burn with them, world without end, in the fire of God's vengeance and the furnace of His wrath.

5. What a sad situation you yourself were in, when Christ concerned Himself for your good. You were going on in the way to hell as blind as a mole. At last Christ opened your eyes and let you see your hazard, by a preacher who was not one of the unconcerned Gallios. He spared neither His body, His credit, nor reputation, to gain you and others like you. Will you then be unconcerned for others?

6. The unconcernedness for the good of souls implies, (I) A dead lifeless heart, a loveless soul, with respect to Christ. If you have any life or love to Christ, do you dare be unconcerned in this matter? Certainly, he who has life will move; and he who has love, will be concerned for the propagating of Christ's kingdom. (2) Especially unbelief of the threatenings of God. If you believe that the wicked shall be turned into hell, and all the nations that forget God, you can not speak to them as if you were telling a story. If you believe that they must depart into everlasting fire, your heart will

not be so frozen as to be unconcerned for them. The sight of it by faith will thaw your frozen heart. (3) A stupid heart, and therefore a hateful attitude. Who would not hate a watchman who saw the enemy coming on, if he should tell the people only in general to get ready to resist their enemies, or should tell them that the enemy were coming on so unconcernedly that they should see he did not care whether they should live or die? And what a hateful stupidity it is in one who carries the gospel to be unconcerned for souls, when they are in such danger?

7. The devil puts to shame such people. He goes about like a roaring lion, seeking whom he may devour; and they, set to keep souls, creep about like a snail. He is in earnest when he tempts; but they are unconcerned whether people hear, or shun to hear their invitations, reproofs, etc. Yes, how concerned are the devil's ministers that do his bidding for him? They will cross over sea and land to gain one proselyte. So shall those who carry the gospel be unconcerned.

8. If it is so that you are unconcerned for the good of souls, it looks like you did not come in by the door, but have broken over the wall, and are only a thief and a robber (John 10:1). *"He that is an hireling, sees the wolf coming, flees, and leaves the sheep, and the wolf catches them."* (vs. 12), *"The hireling flees, because he is an hireling, and does not care for the sheep."* If at any time you find your heart unconcerned then, not having the good of souls before you, remember this.

9. Lastly, you can not expect God's help, if you forget your errand. Have you not known and experienced, that these two, God's help in speaking and a concern for the good of souls, have gone with you at an equal rate.

IV. Christ had not only the good of souls before His eyes, but He was much stirred with their situation; it lay heavy on His spirit. There are these four ways in which this appeared.

1. He had compassion on the multitude, because they were as sheep without a shepherd (Matt. 9:36). That the people lacked true pastors stirred Him; He had compassion on them. Follow Christ in this. Pity those who wander as sheep without a shepherd. And let this move you if you go to preach where congregations have already been planted. You will even see many that are wandering, though they have faithful pastors. Look on them as sheep, and that it is no better for them than if they lacked a shepherd. But especially when you go to those lacking a pastor for a long time, pity them, express compassion for their situation, as sheep lacking a shepherd. Be concerned with their case; and, for this end, consider,

(1) That such people are in a perishing condition: Where this is no vision, the people perish. They are ignorant, and it is no wonder; they have no one to instruct them. They have lean souls, and it is no wonder; they have no one to break the bread of life to them. They wander from God's way;

they have no one to watch over them, and so the devil takes his opportunity.

(2) That for the most part people are deprived of watchmen, because of the bad nature and sensitiveness of their leaders; so that though the people would ever so gladly receive one to break the bread of life to them, yet they cannot get their will, because of these who keep it from them. They simply do not allow them to hear the one who would watch over their souls so that they could call him.

(3) That there are many souls that go out of time into eternity, during the time that they lack a shepherd. Having no one to instruct them, no one to let them see their danger, no one to comfort them when death comes, they slip away, many of them at least, as animals that die.

2. Christ wept, because people in His day did not know, i.e., do, the things that worked for their peace (Luke 19:41,42). When He thought upon this their stupidity, it made the tears trinkle down His precious cheeks. Where are they who are concerned to do what is necessary to be done in order to make their peace with God? Few or none are brought in to Christ. It is rare now to hear of a soul converted, but most are sleeping on in their sins in this day; they like to sit out the day of God's patience with them, until patience is turned into fury. Many heart-melting considerations to this purpose may be found. I shall only say this in general, that such a situation is most deplorable, in the noon day of the time that people should risk a feud with such a dreadful enemy as God is and should sit so quietly even when the sword of vengeance is hanging by a hair over their heads. And they do this notwithstanding that every day may be, for all I know, their last day, and every message may be the last that they ever shall hear. And it may be that before the next day co.nes these enemies shall be made to come face-to-face with the terrible and dreadful Majesty, who shall go through them as thorns and briers and burn them up together by the fire of His wrath, world without end. Can you think of this and not be more concerned with the situation that people are in as they are now-a-days? Surely, if you would weep, here is ground enough for tears of blood.

3. Christ was grieved for the hardness of people's hearts (Mark 3:5). It was reason for grief to the Lord Jesus, that people were so hardened that no means used for their amendment would do them any good. Follow Christ in this. Be grieved and touched with the hardness of the hearts of this generation. Happy are the servants whom God has called out of the vineyard before the ground grow so hard that almost all labor was in vain! This is a time of mourning for those who carry the gospel, for people are strangely hardened. This is even more lamentable if you consider (I) What God has done even for this generation. He has taken off from our necks the yoke of tyranny and arbitrary power, and has given deliverance from

the bondage of bishops appointed for political reasons; and yet in spite of all this the generation is hardened. (2) Consider how the Lord has been dealing with us. For some time there was great dearth of fodder for beasts, yet that did not stir us up. Afterwards was death of cattle; yet we have not returned to the Lord. Then followed death of men, women, and children. He has sent a wind of disease among our grains. This is now, I suppose, the fourth year of our dearth. And in spite of all these things we remain hardened. O Lord, Thou has stricken them, but they have not grieved; Thou has consumed them, but they refuse to receive correction; they make their faces harder than a rock, they refuse to return. What shall be the result of such hardness as this?

(3) It is yet more lamentable, because the plague of hardness seems to be universal. It is not only the wicked, or openly profane, or those that have no religion, but many of the professors of religion that are hardened. This is a day in which the hands of our Moseses are likely to fall, and Amalek is likely to prevail. Many professors desire to hear the causes of God's wrath revealed, but they are not mourning over them; and truly it is most lamentable, that those among us who as so many Joshuas should be discovering the Achans in our camp, who are the troublers of Israel, by a strange kind of dealing are very wary in doing anything about them, or to show them unto people. And it is much to be feared, that there are among us some accursed things that are not yet found out. O that God would put it in the hearts of Zion's watchmen to discover what these Achans are, and that preachers were obliged even by the church to speak more freely of the sins of the land. But, alas, O Lord, why have You hardened all of us from Your fear? (4) This hardness of heart is a token of sad things yet to come. *Who has hardened Himself against God, and prospered?*(Job 10:4). It is a sad prediction of a further blow that because it is clear that we will not be softened either by word or rob, therefore the Lord will thus beat us down further. And knowing this, we may prepare to meet the Lord coming in a way of more severe judgment against us. Spare, O Lord, Your inheritance, Your covenanted people, and make us rather rely on such things as will lead to the removal of the blow.

V. Christ was much in prayer. And He prayed,

1. Before He preached, as Luke 9:18. Follow Him in this. If you preach, you have a great need to pray before you do it. Be busy with God in prayer, when you are thinking on dealing with the souls of men. Let your message be a message of many prayers. Luther said that three things are needed to be a servant of God: persistence, meditation, and prayer. For this purpose consider,

(1) That unless you do this you can not say of your preaching, The Lord says this. How will you get a word from God, if you do not seek it; and how can you seek it except by earnest prayer? If you do something else, you may get something that is the product of your empty head to mumble over before the people. It is miserable preaching where the preacher can

say, Thus say I to you, but no more; and cannot say, The Lord says this.

(2) Consider your own insufficiency and weakness, along with the load of work, Who is sufficient for these things? If you do this you will not dare study without prayer, nor yet pray without study, when God allows you time for both. It is an important work to bring sinners in to Christ, to grab the sticks out of the fire. Don't you have a great need then to be serious with God before you preach?

(3) Consider that word, *"But if they had stood in My counsel, and had caused My people to hear My words, then they should have turned them from their evil way."* (Jer. 23:22). There is no doubt but the fact that there are many who are not standing in God's counsel this day and not making men to hear God's words, is one great reason of the unsuccessfulness of the gospel. Prayer in faith, is the most proper way to become acquainted with the counsel of God. Do not neglect it then.

(4) Lastly, Remember, that whenever you have set aside the Sabbath morning entirely to prayer and meditation you have found the Lord's help in preaching. So this is a good practice. And there are certain things which you should especially keep in mind to pray for;

[1]That you may have a word from the Lord to deliver to the people so that you may not preach to them the product of your own wisdom, and what merely flows from your reason; that is poor, heartless preaching.

[2] That your soul may be touched with the need of the people to whom you preach. If that is lacking, it will be tongue-preaching, but not heart-preaching.

[3]That your heart may be inflamed with zeal for the glory of your Master; that your preaching may flow out of love to God and love to souls.

[4] That the Lord may preach it into your own heart, both when you study and when you deliver it. For if this does not happen, you will be like one who feeds others, but starves himself; or like a road sign that shows the way to men, but never moves a foot itself.

[5] That you may be aided to deliver it; and that you may do it (a) With a proper attitude, your heart being touched with what you yourself speak; (b) Faithfully, holding back nothing that the Lord gives you; and (c) Without confusion of mind, or fear of man.

[6]That you may have physical strength and that your lack of complete health does not bother you.

[7] Lastly, That God would approve you in your work with His presence and power, to make the word spoken a convincing and converting word to those who are out of Christ; to make it a healing word to the broken; and to make it assuring to the weak, doubting, and staggering ones, etc.; that God Himself would drive the fish into the net, when you spread it out. In short, that you may be enabled to commend yourself to God, as a workman that does not need to be ashamed, rightly dividing the word of truth.

2. After preaching, Christ was taken up in prayer. *And when He had sent the multitudes away, He went up into a mountain apart to pray* (Mark 6:46; Matt. 14:23). Follow Christ in this. It is better to do this, than go away with important people in the afternoon. Pray to God, that your labors are not unsuccessful; that what you have delivered, may not be like water spilled on the ground. Pray for pardon for your failings, and that God may accept of your mite which you give with a willing mind, pray that He would not withdraw His blessing because of your failings, but that He would be pleased to water with the dew of heaven the ground in which you sowed the seed, so that it may spring up in due time, and pray that the word that you speak may be like as a nail fastened by the Master of assemblies, so that the devil may not be able to pull it out. Do not think that your work is over and that you have no more to do when the people are dismissed. Oh no, it is not so. The devil was as busy as you were when you were speaking. And afterwards he is not idle. He is working to undo your work, and you must be concerned to hold it together. If a man had a servant that would go out and sow his seed very diligently and faithfully, but would then come in, and sit down idle when it is sown, and forget to harrow it, and cover it with the earth; would the master be well pleased with him? Would he not be highly displeased, because the birds would come and pick it up? So, if you would be oh so much concerned to get good seed and so faithful and diligent in sowing it, yet if afterward you turn careless and do not take time to cover it, the devil may pick it all up. Where is your labor then? How can the Lord be pleased with you? Therefore pray more frequently and try to be as much concerned when it is over, as when you were speaking. There is no doubt, that many times, when you speak some get broken and have convictions of guilt; and some perhaps are strengthened; but both impressions wear off very soon. If your soul were more deeply moved, the weariness of your body would not be so much in your mind; but you would trample on it that you might do good by your work, and souls might not always be robbed by that greedy vulture and roaring lion, the enemy of your own salvation and the salvation of others. Although he has been as busy to do harm all the day to souls, just as you have been to do good, yet he will not complain of weariness at night. Take courage then, and be strong in the Lord. Remember, Christ is concerned for His own seed as well as you. Your Lord and Master had no lack, and there was no fear of His failing in this work of the gospel; yet He prayed, to give all an example. Do not lay aside the pattern then, but follow after His copy even in this.

VI. Christ scorned the world. He slighted it as not suitable for any of His followers. He became poor, that we might become rich (Matt. 8:20). He gave Himself entirely to matters that concerned the calling He had to the work of the gospel (John 9:4). All, especially preachers, are to follow

Christ in the contempt of the world. Yet we must beware of imitating Him in those things which we are not commanded to follow. This does not exempt the preachers of the gospel from providing of things necessary for themselves or others they are concerned in; for the apostle tells us, that he is worse than an infidel, who does not provide for his family (1 Tim. 5:8). Yes, it is clear that the ministers of the gospel may sometimes work with their hands for their living, either when the iniquity of the times in which they live does not allow them what they ought to have, or when taking it will hinder the propagation of the gospel, as is clear by the practice of the apostle Paul. This means that you are not needlessly to involve yourself in worldly matters, to the hindrance of the duties of your calling and position. This is what our Lord teaches us, *Follow Me; and let the dead bury their dead* (Matt. 8:22), and the apostle, *No man that wars entangles himself with the affairs of this life* (2 Tim. 2:4). This was a thing not observed by some, especially bishops, who acted as magistrates as well as ministers; a thing which our Lord absolutely refused. Who made me a judge or a ruler? He said. It is an infallible sign of their ignorance of the importance of their work. Therefore,

1. Beware of preaching to please the people upon getting a call from any church to come. Beware also that the lack of a call does not set you to men-pleasing. That must not be your business. Remember, God provides for you even now as He sees fit. He who took you, and kept you from the womb, will not forsake you but remains faithful. Remember, God has determined the time. Though men and devils should oppose it, they shall not be able to hinder it. It is God Himself that sets the solitary in families; and why should you go out of God's way to get such a thing for yourself. Go on in faithfulness, and do not fear. God can make, yes, will make a man's enemies to be his friends, when his ways please the Lord. And though the corruptions of the people cause them to disapprove of thy teaching and yourself for it, yet their consciences may be made to approve it. And God may bind them up so that they shall not appear to be against you. And what if you should never be settled in any church at all? Christ and His apostles were itinerants. If the Lord sees fit, why should you be against it? If the Lord has something to do with you in diverse corners of His vineyard, calling you sometimes to one place, sometimes to another, you are not to quarrel with that. Perhaps you may do more good that way than in any other. God will always give you food as long as He gives you work; and no matter where you go, you can not go out of your Father's ground. Furthermore, if you should take the other way, and transgress for a piece of bread, you come short of your expectation and lose both the world and a good conscience. But suppose you gain a call from a church and a good salary, and lose a good conscience.

2. Beware that you do not enter into a call on the account of the salary.

See what clearness you can get from the Lord, when any call may come to you, and walk according to His mind. Consider matters drawn out from attention to the salary,

(1) This is direct simony; selling the gift of God for money. Let their money perish with themselves who will risk to do so. Such are buyers and sellers, that God will put out of His temple. Such are mere hirelings, working for wages; and too much of Balaam's temper is to be found there.

(2) It will provoke God to curse your blessings, and to send a moth into that which you may get. And it will surely provoke God to send leanness to your soul, as He did with the Israelites in the wilderness, when He gave them what they were seeking.

(3) You can not expect God's blessing on your labors, but rather that you should be a plague to a people whom you join with in that way. In short, you go in the wrong way and are not approved by God, when you have undertaken the position.

3. There is yet a third case in which contempt or slighting of the world should appear in one sent with the gospel. When a man is settled, and has a salary coming to him, and so has to do worldly business, especially if he is not single, in such a case a minister should endeavor to be involved as little as he can with these things, but shun them as much as lies within him, especially if he has anyone to whom he can trust the management of his affairs. For surely the making of bargains or pursuing them are not the fit object of a minister's employment. I do not mean simply a man may not do that, and yet be a fisher of men; but that many times the man that takes such trouble in the things of the world to catch them, causes himself to be disinclined for the art of man-fishing. But follow Christ in the contempt of the world. You may use it as a staff in your hand, but not as a burden on your back, otherwise the care of souls will not be much in your heart. And to help you in this contempt of the world, consider,

(1) The vanity of the world. Solomon knew well what it was to have abundance, yet he calls all vanity of vanities, all is but vanity. The world is a very empty thing, it cannot comfort the soul under distress. No, the body does you no good when severe ills afflict it. The world cannot be of profit to a man in the day of wrath. A person's riches avail nothing when God arises to plead with him. When he lies down on a death-bed, they can give him no comfort, though all his coffers were full. Why then should such a useless and vain thing be valued so highly?

(2) Love for the world. Where it predominates, it is a sign of lack of love to God: If any man love the world, the love of the Father is not in him. Even in a gracious soul, in so far as the love of the world sways the heart, to that extent the love of God decays. They are as the scales of the balance, as the one goes up, the other goes down.

(3) The uncertainty of worldly things. They are as a bird that takes the wings of the morning, and flees away. How many and various changes in his outward condition are found in a man's life! Men sometimes vile are exalted, honorable men are depressed; and the world is indeed a revolving wheel; that part which is now up, shall before long be down. All things go on in a constant course of unpredictable changes. Nebuchadnezzar in one hour is walking with an uplifted heart in his palace, saying, Is not this great Babylon that I have built, etc? and the next hour he is driven from men, and made to eat grass as an ox. Herod in great pomp makes an oration, the people cry out, It is the voice of a God, and not of a man, and he is immediately eaten up by worms. The rich man today has a good time in luxury, and tomorrow cannot get a drop of water to cool his tongue.

(4)The danger that people are in because of worldly things, when they have more than daily bread. The rich man in Luke 12 felt this to be a stumbling-block on which he broke his neck. The rich young man in the Gospel, because of the love of what he had of the world, parted with Christ, heaven, and glory. Prosperity in the world is a dangerous thing; it is what destroys fools (Prov. 1:32). When Jeshurun grew fat, he kicked against God, and forgot the Lord who fed him (Deut. 32: 15). It was better for David when he was on one side of the hill, and his enemies on the other, and so was in great danger, than when he was walking at ease on his house-top, when he saw Bathsheba. Our Lord tells us, that it is very hard for a rich man to be saved; and teaches us that it is hard to have riches and not set the heart on them. What attention and toil men take to themselves to get them! What anxiety do they have and how they torment themselves to keep them! It exposes men to be the object of others, as Naboth was even for his vineyard; and who can stand before envy? (Prov. 27:4; cf. 1 Tim. 6:9-10). This ruined Naboth (1 Kings 21). He who handles the world, then, can hardly come away with clean fingers. It is a snake in the bosom, that, if God prevent it not by His grace, may sting your soul to death.

5. Remember the shortness and the uncertainty of your life. You are a temporary occupant and you do not know how soon you may move; and you can carry nothing with you. Therefore, if you have food and clothes (which the Lord does not let you lack, be content (1 Tim. 6:7—8). You are a stranger on this earth, going home to your Father's house, where there will be no need of such things as the world affords. Why should you then, desire any more than will carry you to your journey's end? Are you going to set up your tent on this side of Jordan to live here? Are you saying, It is good for me to be here? No, no. You are going homeward, and your Father bids you run and hurry: go then, and take no load on your back; lest it make you stop by the way, and the doors are shut before you reach home, and so you lie outside through the long night of eternity.

Remember that there are other things for you to set your affections on than the things of this world. There are things above that merit your affections. Where is Christ, heaven and glory, when you look upon the world, valuing it highly? Surely the more you see in Him, the less you will see in the world. And hasn't this been confirmed to you by experience? Alas, when the beauty of the upper house is in my offer, that I should ever have any kindness for the world, that disgusting dwarf and monster, that shall at the last be seen by me all in a fire. Behold the King in His glory; look to Him who died for you, to save you from this present evil world. See Him sitting at the right hand of the throne of the Majesty in heaven. Behold the crown in His hand to give you, when you have overcome the world. Behold the recompense of reward bought with His precious blood, if you overcome. Are you looking after toys, and going off your way to gather the stones of the brook, when you should be running for a crown of gold? Is this becoming to a man in his right mind? Doesn't it rather imply insanity and a more than brute stupidity? The animals look down, but men are to look up. They have a soul capable of higher things than what the world affords: therefore, a Latin poem runs,

> While the rest of beasts bend, gazing at the ground,
> God gave to Man a lofty countenance,
> Commanding him to gaze upon the heavens,
> Upright towards the stars to lift his view.

Be then of a more noble spirit than the earthworms. Let the pigs feed on husks. Are you clothed with the sun? Get the moon under your feet then; despise it, do not look on it with love, turn from it, and pass away. Don't let it move you if you are poor. Christ did not have a place to lay His head. Don't let the prospect of future times of distress make you apprehensive how to be carried through; for *you shall not be ashamed in the evil days, and in the days of famine you shall be satisfied* (Psalm 36:19). God said it; therefore believe it. Don't be anxious about providing for your old age, for by all appearance you will never see it. It is more than probable that you will be sooner at your journey's end. The body is weak; it is even stepping down to salute corruption as its mother, before it has well entered the hall of the world: the pins of your tabernacle seem to be drawing out by little and little already. Courage then, for before long the devil, and the world, and the flesh shall be bruised under your feet; and you will be received into eternal mansions. But though the Lord should lengthen out your days to old age, He who brought you into life will not forsake you then either. If He gives you life, He will give you food. Keep a loose hold of the world then; despise it if you would be a fisher of men.

VII. Christ was useful to souls in private conversation, taking occasion to instruct, rebuke, etc., from whatever presented itself. Thus He dealt with the woman of Samaria. He took the opportunity from the water she was drawing to tell her of the living water, etc. When He was at a feast, He rebuked the Pharisees who chose the uppermost seats, instructing them in the right attitude of heart. Follow Christ in this. Be edifying in your private conversation. When you are at any time in company, let something that smells of heaven drop from your lips. Where any are faulty, reprove them as prudently as you can. If they appear to be ignorant, instruct them when need requires, etc. And learn that heavenly chemistry of extracting some spiritual thing out of earthly things. To this purpose and for this end endeavor after a heavenly attitude which will, as is told of the philosopher's stone, turn every metal into gold. When the soul is heavenly, it will even scrape jewels out of a dunghill. Whatever the subject is, it will afford some useful thing or another. O what a shame it is for you to sit down in company, and rise again, and part with them, and never a word of Christ to be heard where you are. Be ashamed of this, and remember what Christ says, *"Whoever shall confess me before men, him I will confess also before my Father – but whoever shall deny me before men, him I will also deny before my Father who is in heaven"* (Matt. 10:32,33).

How many times have you been careful in your conversation when alone, but when in company, by neglect, especially in rebuking, you have come away with loss and a troubled mind, because of your faintheartedness? Reform yourself in this and make your conversation more edifying, and take courage to reprove, exhort, etc. You do not know what a seasonable admonition may do – the Lord may be pleased to back it with life and power.

VIII. Christ laid hold upon opportunities of public preaching when they came about, as is clear from the whole history of the Gospel. He gave a pattern to His servants to be instant in season and out of season. Follow Christ in this. Do not refuse any occasion for preaching when God calls you to it. It is very unlike Christ's practice for preachers of the gospel to be lazy, to slight the opportunities of doing good to a people when the Lord puts opportunities in their hand. For this end consider:

1. Besides Christ's example, that you are worth nothing in the world to the extent that you are lazy; what good do we serve if we are not

2. It may provoke God to take away your talent and give it to another if you are not active. Whatever talent the Lord has given you, it must be employed in His service. He did not give it to you to hide it in a napkin. Remember what became of the unprofitable servant that hid His Lord's money?

3. You know not when your Master will come. And blessed is that servant whom, when His Lord shall come, He shall find so doing. If Christ

should come and find you idle, when He is calling you to work, how will you be able to look Him in the face? They are well that die at Christ's work.

THE END

Words to
Winners of Souls

Horatius Bonar

CONTENTS

" 'Tis not for man to trifle. Life is brief,
    And sin is here.
Our age is but the falling of a leaf—
    A dropping tear.
We have no time to sport away the hours:
All must be earnest in a world like ours.

"Not *many* lives, but only *one* have we,—
    One, only one;
How sacred should that one life ever be—
    That narrow span!
Day after day filled up with blessed toil,
Hour after hour still bringing in new spoil."

I

IMPORTANCE OF A LIVING MINISTRY

"How much more would a few good and fervent men effect in the ministry than a multitude of lukewarm ones!" said Oecolampadius, the Swiss Reformer—a man who had been taught by experience, and who has recorded that experience for the benefit of other churches and other days.

The mere multiplying of men calling themselves ministers of Christ will avail little. They may be but "cumberers of the ground." They may be like Achan, troubling the camp; or perhaps Jonah, raising the tempest. Even when sound in the faith, through unbelief, lukewarmness and slothful formality, they may do irreparable injury to the cause of Christ, freezing and withering up all spiritual life around them. The lukewarm ministry of one who is theoretically orthodox is often more extensively and fatally ruinous to souls than that of one grossly inconsistent or flagrantly heretical. "What man on earth is so pernicious a drone as an idle minister?" said Cecil. And Fletcher remarked well that "lukewarm pastors made careless Christians." Can the multiplication of such ministers, to whatever amount, be counted a blessing to a people?

When the church of Christ, in all her denominations, returns to primitive example, and walking in apostolical footsteps seeks to be conformed more closely to inspired models, allowing nothing that pertains to earth to come between her and her living Head, then will she give more careful heed to see that the men to whom she intrusts the care of souls, however learned and able, should be yet more distinguished by their spirituality, zeal, faith and love.

In comparing Baxter and Orton, the biographer of the former remarks that "Baxter would have set the world on fire while Orton was lighting a match." How true! Yet not true alone of Baxter or of Orton. These two individuals are representatives of two classes in the church of Christ in every age and of every denomination. The latter class are far the more numerous: the Ortons you may count by hundreds, the Baxters by tens; yet who would not prefer a solitary specimen of the one to a thousand of the other?

Baxter's Burning Sincerity

"When he spoke of weighty soul concerns," says one of his contemporaries of Baxter, *"you might find his very spirit drenched therein."* No wonder that he was blessed with such amazing success! Men felt that in listening to him they were in contact with one who was dealing with realities of infinite moment.

This is one of the secrets of ministerial strength and ministerial success. And who can say how much of the overflowing infidelity of the present day is owing not only to the lack of spiritual instructors—not merely to the existence of grossly unfaithful and inconsistent ones—but to the *coldness* of many who are reputed sound and faithful. Men can not but feel that if religion is worth anything, it is worth everything; that if it calls for any measure of zeal and warmth, it will justify the utmost degrees of these; and that there is no consistent medium between reckless atheism and the intensest warmth of religious zeal. Men may dislike, detest, scoff at, persecute the latter, yet their consciences are all the while silently reminding them that if there be a God and a Saviour, a heaven and a hell, anything short of such life and love is hypocrisy, dishonesty, perjury!

And thus the lesson they learn from the lifeless discourses of the class we are alluding to is, that since these men do not believe the doctrines they are preaching there is no need of their hearers believing them; if ministers only believe them because they make their living by them, why should those who make nothing by them scruple about denying them?

"*Rash* preaching," said Rowland Hill, "disgusts; timid preaching leaves poor souls fast asleep; *bold* preaching is the only preaching that is owned of God."

It is not merely unsoundness in faith, nor negligence in duty, nor open inconsistency of life that mars the ministerial work and ruins souls. A man may be free from all scandal either in creed or conduct, and yet may be a most grievous obstruction in the way of all spiritual good to his people. He may be a dry and empty cistern, notwithstanding his orthodoxy. He may be freezing or blasting life at the very time he is speaking of the way of life. He may be repelling men from the cross even when he is in words proclaiming it. He may be standing between his flock and the blessing even when he is, in outward form, lifting up his hand to bless them. The same words that from warm lips would drop as the rain, or distill as the dew, fall from his lips as the snow or hail, chilling all spiritual warmth and blighting all spiritual life. How many souls have been lost for want of earnestness, want of solemnity, want of love in the preacher, even when the words uttered were precious and true!

Our One Object: to Win Souls

We take for granted that the object of the Christian ministry is *to convert sinners and to edify the body of Christ.* No faithful minister can possibly rest short of this. Applause, fame, popularity, honor, wealth—all these are vain. If souls are not won, if saints are not matured, our ministry itself is vain.

The question, therefore, which each of us has to answer to his own conscience is "Has it been the end of my ministry, has it been the desire of my heart to save the lost and guide the saved? Is this my aim in *every sermon* I preach, in every visit I pay? Is it under the influence of this feeling that I continually live and walk and speak? Is it for this I pray and toil and fast and weep? Is it for this I spend and am spent, counting it, next to the salvation of my own soul, my chiefest joy to be the instrument of saving others? Is it for this that I exist? and to accomplish this would I gladly die? Have I seen the pleasure of the Lord prospering in my hand? Have I seen souls converted under my ministry? Have God's people found refreshment from my lips, and gone upon their way rejoicing? or have I seen no fruit of my labors, and yet am I content to remain unblest? Am I satisfied to preach, and yet not know of one saving impression made, one sinner awakened?"

Nothing short of positive success can satisfy a true minister of Christ. His plans may proceed smoothly and his external machinery may work steadily, but without actual fruit in the saving of souls he counts all these as nothing. His feeling is, "My little children, of whom I travail in birth again, until Christ be formed in you." And it is this feeling which makes him successful.

"Ministers," said Owen, "are seldom honored with success unless they are continually aiming at the conversion of sinners." The resolution that in the strength and with the blessing of God he will never rest without success, will insure it. It is the man who has made up his mind to confront every difficulty, who has counted the cost and, fixing his eye upon the prize, has determined to fight his way to it—it is such a man that conquers.

The dull apathy of other days is gone. Satan has taken the field actively, and it is best to meet him front to front. Besides, men's consciences are really on edge. God seems extensively striving with them, as before the flood. A breath of the Divine Spirit has passed over the earth, and hence the momentous character of the time, as well as the necessity for improving it so long as it lasts.*

---

* Bonar's comments on spiritual conditions in his day (1859) are strikingly appropriate for the present.

The one true goal or resting-place where doubt and weariness, the stings of a pricking conscience, and the longings of an unsatisfied soul would all be quieted, is *Christ himself*. Not the church, but Christ. Not doctrine, but Christ. Not forms, but Christ. Not ceremonies, but Christ; Christ the God-man, giving His life for ours; sealing the everlasting covenant, and making peace for us through the blood of His cross; Christ the divine storehouse of all light and truth, "in whom are hid all the treasures of wisdom and knowledge"; Christ the infinite vessel, filled with the Holy Spirit, the Enlightener, the Teacher, the Quickener, the Comforter, so that "out of His fullness we may receive, and grace for grace." This, this alone is the vexed soul's refuge, its rock to build on, its home to abide in till the great tempter be bound and every conflict ended in victory.

Meet "Opinion" With the Truth

Let us, then, meet this "earnestness" which is now the boast, but may ere long be the bane, of the age, with that which alone can bring down its feverish pulse, and soothe it into blessed calm, "the gospel of the grace of God." All other things are but opiates, drugs, quackeries; this is the divine medicine; this is the sole, the speedy, the eternal cure. It is not by "opinion" that we are to meet "opinion"; it is the *Truth of God* that we are to wield; and applying the *edge* of the "sword of the Spirit" to the theories of man (which he proudly calls his "opinions"), make him feel what a web of sophistry and folly he has been weaving for his own entanglement and ruin.

It is not opinions that man needs: it is *Truth*. It is not theology: it is *God*. It is not religion: it is *Christ*. It is not literature and science; but the knowledge of the free love of God in the gift of His only-begotten Son.

"I know not," says Richard Baxter, "what others think, but for my own part I am ashamed of my stupidity, and wonder at myself that I deal not with my own and others' souls as one that looks for the great day of the Lord; and that I can have room for almost any other thoughts and words; and that such astonishing matters do not wholly absorb my mind. I marvel how I can preach of them slightly and coldly; and how I can let men alone in their sins; and that I do not go to them, and beseech them, for the Lord's sake, to repent, however they may take it, and whatever pain and trouble it should cost me.

"I seldom come out of the pulpit but my conscience smiteth me that I have been no more serious and fervent. It accuseth me not so much for want of ornaments and elegancy, nor for letting fall an unhandsome word; but it asketh me, 'How couldst thou speak of life and death with such a heart? How couldst thou preach of heaven and hell in such a careless, sleepy manner? Dost thou believe what thou sayest? Art thou in earnest, or in jest? How canst thou tell people that sin is such a thing, and that so much misery is upon them and before them, and be no more affected with it? Shouldst thou not weep over such a people, and should not thy tears interrupt thy words? Shouldst thou not cry aloud, and show them their transgressions; and entreat and beseech them as for life and death?'

"Truly this is the peal that conscience doth ring in my ears, and yet my drowsy soul will not be awakened. Oh, what a thing is an insensible, hardened heart! O Lord, save us from the plague of infidelity and hardheartedness ourselves, or else how shall we be fit instruments of saving others from it? Oh, do that on our souls which thou wouldst use us to do on the souls of others!"

II

THE MINISTER'S TRUE
LIFE AND WALK

The *true* minister must be a *true* Christian. He must be called
by God before he can call others to God. The Apostle Paul
thus states the matter: "God hath reconciled us to himself by
Jesus Christ, and hath given to us the ministry of reconciliation." They were first reconciled, and then they had given to
them the ministry of reconciliation. Are we *ministers* reconciled? It is but reasonable that a man who is to act as a spiritual guide to others should himself know the way of salvation.
It has been frequently said that "the way to heaven is blocked
up with dead professors"; but is it not true also that the melancholy obstruction is not composed of *members* of churches only?
Let us take heed unto ourselves!

As the minister's life is in more than one respect the life of a
ministry, let us speak a few words on ministerial holy living.

Let us seek the Lord *early*. "If my heart be early seasoned
with his presence, it will savor of him all day after." Let us see
God before man every day. "I ought to pray before seeing any
one. Often when I sleep long, or meet with others early, and
then have family prayer and breakfast and forenoon callers, it
is eleven or twelve o'clock before I begin secret prayer. This
is a wretched system. It is unscriptural. Christ rose before day,
and went into a solitary place. . . Family prayer loses much of
power and sweetness, and I can do no good to those who come
to seek for me. The conscience feels guilty, the soul unfed, the
lamp not trimmed. Then, when secret prayer comes, the soul is
often out of tune. I feel it far better to begin with God, to see
his face first, to get my soul near Him before it is near another.

13

. . . It is best to have at least one hour *alone with God* before engaging in anything else. At the same time, I must be careful not to reckon communion with God by minutes or hours, or by solitude." (M'Cheyne.)

Hear this true servant of Christ exhorting a beloved brother: "Take heed to *thyself*. Your own soul is your first and greatest care. You know a sound body alone can work with power, much more a *healthy soul*. Keep a clear conscience through the blood of the Lamb. Keep up close communion with God. Study likeness to Him in all things. Read the Bible for your own growth first, then for your people."

"With him," says his biographer, "the commencement of all labor invariably consisted in the preparation of his own soul. The forerunner of each day's visitations was a calm season of private devotion during morning hours. The walls of his chamber were witnesses of his prayerfulness—I believe of his tears as well as of his cries. The pleasant sound of psalms often issued from his room at an early hour; then followed the reading of the Word for his own sanctification: and few have so fully realized the blessing of the first psalm." Would that it were so with us all! "Devotion," said Bishop Hall, "is the life of religion, the very soul of piety, the highest employment of grace." It is much to be feared that "we are weak in the pulpit because we are weak in the closet." (James.)

"Walking With God"

"To restore a commonplace truth," writes Mr. Coleridge, "to its first uncommon luster, you need only translate it into action." *Walking with God* is a very commonplace truth. Translate this truth into action—how lustrous it becomes! The phrase, how hackneyed!—the thing, how rare! It is such a walk —not an abstract ideal, but a personality, a life—which the reader is invited to contemplate. Oh, that we would only set ourselves in right earnest to this rare work of translation!

It is said of the energetic, pious and successful John Berridge that "communion with God was what he enforced in the latter stages of his ministry. It was, indeed, his own meat and drink, and the banquet from which he never appeared to rise." This shows us the source of his great strength. If we were always sitting at this banquet, then it might be recorded of us ere long, as of him, "He was in the first year visited by about a thousand persons under serious impressions."

Study the Speakers, Not the Sermons

To the *men* even more than to their doctrine we would point the eye of the inquirer who asks, Whence came their success? and Why may not the same success be ours? We may take the sermons of Whitefield or Berridge or Edwards for our study or our pattern, but it is the individuals themselves that we must mainly set before us; it is with the spirit of the men, more than of their works, that we are to be imbued, if we are emulous of a ministry as powerful, as victorious as theirs. They were spiritual men, and walked with God. It is living fellowship with a living Saviour which, transforming us into His image, fits us for being able and successful ministers of the gospel.

Without this nothing else will avail. Neither orthodoxy, nor learning, nor eloquence, nor power of argument, nor zeal, nor fervor, will accomplish aught without this. It is this that gives power to our words and persuasiveness to our arguments, making them either as the balm of Gilead to the wounded spirit or as sharp arrows of the mighty to the conscience of the stout-hearted rebel. From them that walk with Him in holy, happy intercourse, a virtue seems to go forth, a blessed fragrance seems to compass them whithersoever they go. Nearness to Him, intimacy with Him, assimiliation to His character—these are the elements of a ministry of power.

When we can tell our people, "We beheld His glory, and therefore we speak of it; it is not from report we speak, but we have *seen* the King in His beauty"—how lofty the position we occupy! Our power in drawing men to Christ springs chiefly from the fulness of our personal joy in Him, and the nearness of our personal communion with Him. The countenance that reflects most of Christ, and shines most with His love and grace, is most fitted to attract the gaze of a careless, giddy world, and win restless souls from the fascinations of creature-love and creature-beauty. A ministry of power must be the fruit of a holy, peaceful, loving intimacy with the Lord.

Faithfulness Essential to Success

"The law of truth was in his mouth, and iniquity was not found in his lips: he walked with me in peace and equity, and did turn many away from iniquity" (Malachi 2:6). Let us observe the connection here declared to subsist between faithfulness and success in the work of the ministry; between a godly life and the "turning away many from iniquity." The end for which we first took office, as we declared at ordination, was the *saving of souls;* the end for which we still live and labor is the same; the means to this end are a holy life and a faithful fulfillment of our ministry.

The connection between these two things is close and sure. We are entitled to calculate upon it. We are called upon to pray and labor with the confident expectation of its being realized; and where it is not, to examine ourselves with all diligence, lest the cause of the failure be found in ourselves; in our want of faith, love, prayer, zeal and warmth, spirituality and holiness of life; for it is by these that the Holy Spirit is grieved away. Success is attainable; success is desirable; success is promised by God; and nothing on earth can be bitterer to the soul of a faithful minister than the want of it. To walk with God, and to be faithful to our trust, is declared to be the certain way of attaining it. Oh, how much depends on the holiness of our life, the consistency of our character, the heavenliness of our walk and conversation!

Our position is such that we can not remain neutral. Our life can not be one of harmless obscurity. We must either repel or attract—save or ruin souls! How loud, then, the call, how strong the motive, to spirituality of soul and circumspectness of life! How solemn the warning against worldly-mindedness and vanity,—against levity and frivolity,—against negligence and sloth and cold formality!

Of all men, a minister of Christ is especially called to walk with God. Everything depends on this; his own peace and joy, his own future reward at the coming of the Lord. But especially does God point to this as the true and sure way of securing the blessing. This is the grand secret of ministerial success. One who walks with God reflects the light of His countenance upon a benighted world; and the closer he walks, the more of this light does he reflect. One who walks with God carries in his very air and countenance a sweet serenity and holy joy that diffuses tranquility around. One who walks with God receives and imparts life whithersoever he goes; as it is written, "Out of him shall flow rivers of living water." He is not merely the world's light but the world's fountain, dispensing the water of life on every side and making the barren waste to blossom as the rose. He waters the world's wilderness as he moves along his peaceful course. His life is blessed; his example is blessed; his intercourse is blessed; his words are blessed; his ministry is blessed! Souls are saved, sinners are converted, and many are turned from their iniquity.

III

PAST DEFECTS

"O my God, I am ashamed and blush to lift up my face to thee, my God . . . O our God, what shall we say after this?"—EZRA 9:6,10.

To deliver sermons on each returning Lord's Day, to administer the Lord's Supper statedly, to pay an occasional visit to those who request it, to attend religious meetings—this, we fear, sums up the ministerial life of multitudes who are, by profession, overseers of the flock of Christ. An incumbency of thirty, forty or fifty years often yields no more than this. So many sermons, so many baptisms, so many sacraments, so many visits, so many meetings of various kinds—these are all the pastoral annals, the parish records, the ALL of a lifetime's ministry to many! Of *souls* that have been saved, such a record could make no mention.

Mulitudes have perished under such a ministry; the judgment only will disclose whether so much as one has been saved. There might be learning, but there was no "tongue of the learned to speak a word in season to him that is weary." There might be wisdom, but it certainly was not the wisdom that "winneth souls." There might even be the sound of the gospel, but it seemed to contain no glad tidings at all; it was not sounded forth from warm lips into startled ears as the message of eternal life—"the glorious gospel of the blessed God." Men lived, and it was never asked of them by their minister whether they were born again! Men sickened, sent for the minister and received a prayer upon their death-beds as their passport into heaven. Men died, and were buried where all their fathers had been laid; there was a prayer at their funeral, and decent respects to their remains; but their souls went up to the judgment-seat unthought of, uncared for; no man, not even the minister who had vowed to watch for them, having said to them, Are you ready?—or warned them to flee from the wrath to come.

Is not this description too true of many a district and many a minister? We do not speak in anger; we do not speak in scorn: we ask the question solemnly and earnestly. It needs an answer. If ever there was a time when there should be "great searching of heart" and frank acknowledgment of unfaithfulness, it is now when God is visiting us—visiting us both in judgment and mercy. We speak in brotherly kindness; surely the answer should not be of wrath and bitterness. And if this description be true, what sin must there be in ministers and people! How great must be the spiritual desolation that prevails! Surely there is something in such a case grievously wrong; something which calls for solemn self-examination in every minister; something which requires deep repentance.

The Tragedy of a Barren Ministry

Fields plowed and sown, yet yielding no fruit! Machinery constantly in motion, yet all without one particle of produce! Nets cast into the sea, and spread wide, yet no fishes inclosed! All this for years—for a lifetime! How strange! Yet it is true. There is neither fancy nor exaggeration in the matter. Question some ministers—and what other account can they give? They can tell you of sermons *preached,* but of sermons *blest* they can say nothing. They can speak of discourses that were admired and praised, but of discourses that have been made effectual by the Holy Spirit they can not speak. They can tell you how many have been baptized, how many communicants admitted; but of souls awakened, converted, ripening in grace, they can give no account. They can enumerate the sacraments they have dispensed; but as to whether any of them have been "times of refreshing" or times of awakening, they can not say. They can tell you what and how many cases of discipline have passed through their hands; but whether any of these have issued in godly sorrow for sin, whether the professed penitents who were absolved by them gave evidence of being "washed and sanctified and justified," they can give no information; they never thought of such an issue!

They can tell what is the attendance at school, and what are the abilities of the teacher; but how many of these precious little ones whom they have vowed to feed are seeking the Lord they know not; or whether their teacher be a man of prayer and piety they can not say. They can tell you the population of their parish, the number of their congregation, or the temporal condition of their flocks; but as to their spiritual state, how many have been awakened from the sleep of death, how many are followers of God as dear children, they can not pretend to say. Perhaps they would deem it rashness and presumption, if not fanaticism, to inquire. And yet they have sworn, before men and angels, to *watch for their souls* as they that must give account! But oh, of what use are sermons, sacraments, schools, if *souls* are left to perish; if living religion be lost sight of; if the Holy Spirit be not sought; if men are left to grow up and die unpitied, unprayed for, unwarned!

For God's Glory and Man's Good

It was not so in other days. Our fathers really watched and preached for souls. They asked and they expected a blessing. Nor were they denied it. They were blessed in turning many to righteousness. Their lives record their successful labors. How refreshing the lives of those who lived only for the glory of God and the good of souls. There is something in their history that compels us to feel that they were ministers of Christ—true watchmen.

How cheering to read of Baxter and his labors at Kidderminster! How solemn to hear of Venn and his preaching, in regard to which it is said that men "fell before him like slaked lime"! And in the much-blest labors of that man of God, the apostolic Whitefield, is there not much to humble us, as well as to stimulate? Of Tanner, who was himself awakened under Whitefield, we read that he "seldom preached one sermon in vain." Of Berridge and Hicks we are told that in their missionary tours throughout England they were blessed in one year to awaken four thousand souls. Oh, for these days again! Oh, for one day of Whitefield again!

Thus one has written—"The language we have been accustomed to adopt is this; we must use the means, and leave the event to God; we can do no more than employ the means; this is our duty and having done this we must leave the rest to Him who is the disposer of all things. Such language sounds well, for it seems to be an acknowledgment of our own nothingness, and to savor of submission to God's sovereignty; but it is only sound—it has not really any substance in it, for though there is truth stamped on *the face* of it, there is falsehood at *the root* of it. To talk of submission to God's sovereignty is one thing, but really to submit to it is another and quite different thing.

Submission Involves Renunciation

"Really to submit to God's sovereign disposal does always necessarily involve the deep renunciation of our own will in the matter concerned, and such a renunciation of the will can never be effected without a soul being brought through very severe and trying exercises of an inward and most humbling nature. Therefore, whilst we are quietly satisfied in using the means without obtaining the end, and this costs us no such painful inward exercise and deep humbling as that alluded to, if we think that we are leaving the affair to God's disposal—we deceive ourselves, and the truth in this matter is not in us.

"No; really to give anything to God implies that *the will,* which is emphatically *the heart,* has been *set on that thing;* and if *the heart* has indeed been *set* on the salvation of sinners as the end to be answered by the means we use, we can not possibly give up that end without, as was before observed, the heart being severely exercised and deeply pained by the renunciation of the will involved in it. When, therefore, we can be quietly content to use the means for saving souls without seeing them saved thereby, it is because there is no renunciation of the will—that is, no real giving up to God in the affair. The fact is, the will—that is, *the heart*—had never really been set upon this end; if it had, it could not possibly give up such an end without being *broken* by the sacrifice.

"When we can thus be satisfied to use the means without obtaining the end, and speak of it as though we were submitting to the Lord's disposal, we use a truth to hide a falsehood, exactly in the same way that those formalists in religion do, who continue in forms and duties without going beyond them, though they know they will not save them, and who, when they are warned of their danger and earnestly entreated to seek the Lord with all the heart, reply by telling us they know they must repent and believe but that they can not do either the one or the other of themselves and that they must wait till God gives them grace to do so. Now, this is a truth, absolutely considered; yet most of us can see that they are using it as a falsehood to cover and excuse a great insincerity of heart. We can readily perceive that if their hearts were really set upon salvation, they could not rest satisfied without it. Their contentedness is the result, not of heart-submission to God, but in reality of *heart-indifference to the salvation of their own souls.*

Covering Falsehood With Truth

"Exactly so it is with us as ministers: when we can rest satisfied with using the means for saving souls without seeing them really saved, or we ourselves being broken-hearted by it, and at the same time quietly talk of leaving the event to God's disposal, we make use of a truth to cover and excuse a falsehood;

for our ability to leave the matter thus is not, as we imagine, the result of heart-submission to God, but of heart-indifference to the salvation of the souls we deal with. No, truly, if the heart is really set on such an end, it must gain that end or break in losing it."

He that saved our souls has taught us to weep over the unsaved. Lord, let that mind be in us that was in Thee! Give us thy tears to weep; for, Lord, our hearts are hard toward our fellows. We can see thousands perish around us, and our sleep never be disturbed; no vision of their awful doom ever scaring us, no cry from their lost souls ever turning our peace into bitterness.

Our families, our schools, our congregations, not to speak of our cities at large, our land, our world, might well send us daily to our knees; for the loss of even *one soul* is terrible beyond conception. Eye has not seen, nor ear heard, nor has entered the heart of man, what a soul in hell must suffer forever. Lord, give us bowels of mercies! "What a mystery! The soul and eternity of one man depends upon the voice of another!"

IV

MINISTERIAL CONFESSION

"Remember therefore from whence thou art fallen, and repent, and do the first works; or else I will come unto thee quickly, and will remove thy candlestick out of his place, except thou repent."

—REVELATION 2:5.

In the year 1651 the Church of Scotland, feeling in regard to her ministers "how deep their hand was in the transgression, and that ministers had no small accession to the drawing on of the judgments that were upon the land," drew up what they called a humble acknowledgment of the sins of the ministry. This document is a striking and searching one. It is perhaps one of the fullest, most faithful and most impartial confessions of ministerial sin ever made. A few extracts from it will suitably introduce this chapter on ministerial confession. It begins with confessing sins before entrance on the ministry:

"Lightness and profanity in conversation, unsuitable to that holy calling which they did intend, not thoroughly repented of. Not studying to be in Christ before they be in the ministry; nor to have the practical knowledge and experience of the mystery of the gospel in themselves before they preach it to others. Neglecting to fit themselves for the work of the ministry, in not improving prayer and fellowship with God, opportunities of a lively ministry, and other means, and not mourning for these neglects. Not studying self-denial, nor resolving to take up the cross of Christ. Negligence to entertain a sight and sense of sin and misery; not wrestling against corruption, nor studying mortification and subduedness of spirit."

Of entrance on the ministry it thus speaks:

"Entering to the ministry without respect to a commission from Jesus Christ, by which it hath come to pass that many have run unsent. Entering to the ministry not from the love of Christ, nor from a desire to honor God in gaining of souls, but for a name and for a livelihood in the world notwithstanding a solemn declaration to the contrary at admission."

Of the sins after entrance on the ministry, it thus searchingly enumerates:

"Ignorance of God; want of nearness with Him, and taking up little of God in reading, meditating and speaking of Him. Exceeding great selfishness in all that we do; acting from ourselves, for ourselves and to ourselves. Not caring how unfaithful and negligent others were, so being it might contribute a testimony to our faithfulness and diligence, but being rather content, if not rejoicing, at their faults. Least delight in those things wherein lieth our nearest communion with God; great inconstancy in our walk with God, and neglect of acknowledging Him in all our ways. In going about duties, least careful of those things which are most remote from the eyes of men. Seldom in secret prayer with God, except to fit for public performance; and even that much neglected, or gone about very superficially.

Glad to Find Excuses

"Glad to find excuses for the neglect of duties. Neglecting the reading of Scriptures in secret, for edifying ourselves as Christians; only reading them in so far as may fit us for our duty as ministers, and ofttimes neglecting that. Not given to reflect upon our own ways, nor allowing conviction to have a thorough work upon us; deceiving ourselves by resting upon absence from and abhorrence of evils from the light of a natural conscience, and looking upon the same as an evidence of a real change of state and nature. Evil guarding of and watching over the heart, and carelessness in self-searching; which makes much unacquaintedness with ourselves and estrangedness from God. Not guarding nor wrestling against seen and known evils, especially our predominants. A facility to be drawn away with the temptations of the time, and other particular temptations, according to our inclinations and fellowship.

"Instability and wavering in the ways of God, through the fears of persecutions, hazard, or loss of esteem; and declining duties because of the fear of jealousies and reproaches. Not esteeming the cross of Christ, and sufferings for His name, honorable, but rather shifting sufferings, from self-love. Deadness of spirit, after all the sore strokes of God upon the land. Little conscience made of secret humiliation and fasting, by ourselves apart and in our families, that we might mourn for our own and the land's guiltiness and great backslidings; and little applying of public humiliation to our own hearts. Finding of our own pleasure, when the Lord calls for our humiliation.

"Not laying to heart the sad and heavy sufferings of the people of God abroad, and the not-thriving of the kingdom of Jesus Christ and the power of godliness among them. Refined hypocrisy; desiring to appear what, indeed, we are not. Studying more to learn the language of God's people than their exercise. Artificial confessing of sin, without repentance; professing to declare iniquity, and not resolving to be sorry for sin. Confession in secret much slighted, even of those things whereof we are convicted. No reformation, after solemn acknowledgments and private vows; thinking ourselves exonerated after confession. Readier to search out and censure faults in others than to see or deal with them in ourselves. Accounting of our estate and way according to the estimation that others have of us. Estimation of men, as they agree with or disagree from us.

"Not fearing to meet with trials, but presuming, in our own strength, to go through them unshaken. Not learning to fear, by the falls of gracious men; nor mourning and praying for them. Not observing particular deliverances and punishments; not improving of them, for the honor of God, and the edification of ourselves and others. Little or no mourning for the corruption of our nature, and less groaning under, and longing to be delivered from, that body of death, the bitter root of all our other evils.

"Fruitless conversing ordinarily with others, for the worse rather than for the better. Foolish jesting away of time with impertinent and useless discourse, very unbecoming the ministers of the gospel. Spiritual purposes often dying in our hands when they are begun by others. Carnal familiarity with natural, wicked and malignant men, whereby they are hardened, the people of God stumbled, and we ourselves blunted.

Loving Pleasure More than God

"Slighting of fellowship with those by whom we might profit. Desiring more to converse with those that might better us by their talents than with such as might edify us by their graces. Not studying opportunities of doing good to others. Shifting of prayer and other duties, when called thereto—choosing rather to omit the same than that we should be put to them ourselves. Abusing of time in frequent recreation and pastimes and loving our pleasures more than God. Taking little or no time to Christian discourse with young men trained up for the ministry. Common and ordinary discourse on the Lord's Day. Slighting Christian admonition from any of our flocks or others, as being below us; and ashamed to take light and warning from private Christians. Dislike of, or bitterness against, such as deal freely with us by admonition or reproof, and not dealing faithfully with others who would welcome it off our hands.

"Not praying for men of a contrary judgment, but using reservedness and distance from them; being more ready to speak *of* them than *to* them or to God *for* them. Not weighed with the failings and miscarriages of others, but rather taking advantage thereof for justifying ourselves. Talking of and sporting at the faults of others, rather than compassionating of them. No due painstaking in religious ordering of our families, nor studying to be patterns to other families in the government of ours. Hasty anger and passion in our families and conversation with others. Covetousness, worldly-mindedness, and an inordinate desire after the things of this life, upon which followeth a neglect of the duties of our calling, and our being taken up for the most part with the things of the world. Want of hospitality and charity to the members of Christ. Not cherishing godliness in the people; and some being afraid of it and hating the people of God for piety, and studying to bear down and quench the work of the Spirit amongst them.

Trusting in Our Own Ability

"Not entertaining that edge of spirit in ministerial duties which we found at the first entry to the ministry. Great neglect of reading, and other preparation; or preparation merely literal and bookish, making an idol of a book, which hindereth communion with God; or presuming on bygone assistance, and praying little. Trusting to gifts, talents, and pains taken for preparation, whereby God is provoked to blast good matter, well ordered and worded. Careless in employing Christ, and drawing virtue out of Him, for enabling us to preach in the Spirit and in the power. In praying for assistance we pray more for assistance to the messenger than to the message which we carry, not caring what becomes of the Word, if we be with some measure of assistance carried on in the duty. The matter we bring forth is not seriously recommended to God by prayer, to be quickened to His people. Neglect of prayer after the Word is preached.

"Neglect to warn, in preaching, of snares and sins in public affairs by some; and too much, too frequent, and unnecessary speaking by others of public business and transactions. Exceeding great neglect and unskillfulness to set forth the excellences and usefulness of (and the necessity of an interest in) Jesus Christ, and the new covenant, which ought to be the great subject of a minister's study and preaching. Speaking of Christ more by hearsay than from knowledge and experience, or any real impression of Him upon the heart. The way of most ministers' preaching too legal. Want of sobriety in preaching the gospel; not savoring anything but what is new; so that the substantials of religion bear but little bulk.

"Not preaching Christ in the simplicity of the gospel, nor ourselves the people's servants, for Christ's sake. Preaching of Christ, not that the people may know Him, but that they may think we know much of Him. Preaching about Christ's leaving of the world without brokenness of heart, or stirring up of ourselves to take hold of Him. Not preaching with bowels of compassion to them that are in hazard to perish. Preaching against public sins, neither in such a way, nor for such an end, as we ought—for the gaining of souls and drawing men out of their sins; but rather because it is to our advantage to say something of these evils.

Attitude Toward Our Opponents

"Bitterness, instead of zeal, in speaking against malignants, sectarians, and other scandalous persons; and unfaithfulness therein. Not studying to know the particular condition of the souls of the people, that we may speak to them accordingly; nor keeping a particular record thereof, though convinced of the usefulness of this. Not carefully choosing what may be most profitable and edifying; and want of wisdom in application to the several conditions of souls; not so careful to bring home the point by application as to find out the doctrine, nor speaking the same with that reverence which becomes His word and message.

"Choosing texts whereon we have something to say, rather than those suited to the conditions of souls and times, and frequent preaching of the same things, that we may not be put to the pains of new study. Such a way of reading, preaching and prayer as puts us in these duties farther from God. Too soon satisfied in the discharge of duties, and holding off challenges of conscience with excuses. Indulging the body, and wasting much time idly. Too much eyeing our own credit and applause; and being pleased with it when we get it, and unsatisfied when it is wanting. Timorousness in delivering God's message; letting people die in reigning sins without warning. Studying the discharge of duties rather to free ourselves from censure than to approve ourselves to God.

"Not making all the counsel of God known to His people; and particularly, not giving testimony in times of defection. Not studying to profit by our own doctrine, nor the doctrine of others. For most part, preaching as if we ourselves were not concerned in the message which we carry to the people. Not rejoicing at the conversion of sinners, but content with the unthriving of the Lord's work amongst His people, as suiting best with our minds; fearing, if they should thrive better, we should be more put to it, and less esteemed of by them—many, in preaching and practice, bearing down the power of godliness. We preach not as before God, but as to men; as doth appear by the different pains in our preparation to speak to our ordinary hearers and to others to whom we would approve ourselves.

"Negligent, lazy, and partial visiting of the sick. If they be poor we go once, and only when sent for; if they be rich and of better note, we go oftener and unsent for. Not knowing how to speak with the tongue of the learned a word in season to the weary.

"Lazy and negligent in catechising. Not preparing our hearts before, nor wrestling with God for a blessing to it, because of the ordinariness and apprehended easiness of it; whereby the Lord's name is much taken in vain, and the people little profited. Looking on that exercise as a work below us, and not condescending to study a right and profitable way of instructing the Lord's people. Partial in catechising, passing by those that are rich and of better quality, though many of such stand ordinarily in great need of instruction. Not waiting upon and following the ignorant but often passionately upbraiding them."

These are solemn confessions—the confessions of men who knew the nature of that ministry on which they had entered, and who were desirous of approving themselves to Him who had called them, that they might give in their account with joy and not with grief.

Confessing Our Shortcomings

Let us, as they did, deal honestly with ourselves. Our confessions ought to be no less ample and searching.

1. *We have been unfaithful.* The fear of man and the love of his applause have often made us afraid. We have been unfaithful to our own souls, to our flocks, and to our brethren; unfaithful in the pulpit, in visiting, in discipline, in the church. In the discharge of every one of the duties of our stewardship there has been grievous unfaithfulness. Instead of the special particularization of the sin reproved, there has been the vague allusion. Instead of the bold reproof, there has been the timid hint. Instead of the uncompromising condemnation, there has been the feeble disapproval. Instead of the unswerving consist-

ency of a holy life whose uniform tenor should be a protest against the world and a rebuke of sin, there has been such an amount of unfaithfulness in our walk and conversation, in our daily deportment and intercourses with others, that any degree of faithfulness we have been enabled to manifest on the Lord's Day is almost neutralized by the want of circumspection which our weekday life exhibits.

Archbishop Ussher's Example

Few men ever lived a life so busy and so devoted to God as Ussher, Archbishop of Armagh. His learning, habits of business, station, friends, all contributed to keep his hands every moment full; and then his was a soul that seemed continually to hear a voice saying: "Redeem the time, for the days are evil." Early, too, did he begin, for at ten years of age he was hopefully converted by a sermon preached on Romans 12:1: "I beseech you therefore, brethren, by the mercies of God, that ye present your bodies a living sacrifice." He was a painstaking, laborious preacher of the Word for fifty-five years.

Yet hear him on his death-bed! How he clings to Christ's righteousness alone, and sees in himself, even after such a life, only sin and want. The last words he was heard to utter were about one o'clock in the afternoon, and these words were uttered in a loud voice—*"But, Lord, in special forgive me my sins of omission."* It was *omissions,* says his biographer, he begged forgiveness of with his most fervent last breath—he who was never known to omit an hour, but who employed the shred ends of his life for his great Lord and Master! The very day he took his last sickness, he rose up from writing one of his great works and went out to visit a sick woman, to whom he spoke so fitly and fully that you would have taken him to have spoken of heaven before he came there. Yet this man was oppressed with a sense of his *omissions!*

Reader, what think you of yourself—your undone duties,

your unimproved hours, times of prayer omitted, your shrinking from unpleasant work and putting it on others, your being content to sit under your vine and fig tree without using all efforts for the souls of others? *"Lord, in special forgive me my sins of omission!"*

Hear the confession of Edwards, in regard both to personal and ministerial sins: "Often I have had very affecting views of my own sinfulness and vileness; very frequently to such a degree as to hold me in a kind of loud weeping, sometimes for a considerable time together, so that I have often been forced to shut myself up. I have had a vastly greater sense of my own wickedness, and the badness of my heart, than ever I had before my conversion. My wickedness, as I am in myself, has long appeared to me perfectly ineffable, swallowing up all thought and imagination. I know not how to express better what my sins appear to me to be than by heaping infinite upon infinite, and multiplying infinite by infinite. When I look into my heart and take a view of my wickedness, it looks like an abyss infinitely deeper than hell. And yet it seems to me that my conviction of sin is exceedingly small and faint: it is enough to amaze me that I have no more sense of my sin. I have greatly longed of late for a broken heart, and to lie low before God."

Worldliness Stunts the Conscience

2. *We have been carnal and unspiritual.** The tone of our life has been low and earthly. Associating too much and too intimately with the world, we have in a great measure become accustomed to its ways. Hence our tastes have been vitiated, our consciences blunted, and that sensitive tenderness of feeling which, while it turns not back from suffering yet shrinks from the remotest contact with sin, has worn off and given place to

---

* "Our want of usefulness is much oftener to be ascribed to our want of spirituality than to any want of natural ability."—*Fuller.* "I see that spirituality of mind is the main qualification for the work of the ministry."—*Urquhart.*

an amount of callousness of which we once, in fresher days, believed ourselves incapable.

Perhaps we can call to mind a time when our views and aims were fixed upon a standard of almost unearthly elevation, and, contrasting these with our present state, we are startled at the painful changes. And besides intimacy with the world, other causes have operated in producing this deterioration in the spirituality of our minds. The study of truth in its dogmatical more than in its devotional form has robbed it of its freshness and power; daily, hourly occupation in the routine of ministerial labor has engendered formality and coldness; continual employment in the most solemn duties of our office, such as dealing with souls in private about their immortal welfare, or guiding the meditations and devotions of God's assembled people, or handling the sacramental symbols—this, gone about often with so little prayer and mixed with so little faith, has tended grievously to divest us of that profound reverence and godly fear which ever ought to possess and pervade us. How truly, and with what emphasis, we may say: "We are carnal, sold under sin." The world has not been crucified to us, nor we unto the world; the flesh, with its members, has not been mortified. What a sad effect all this has had, not only upon our peace of soul, on our growth in grace, but upon the success of our ministry!

3. *We have been selfish.* We have shrunk from toil, difficulty and endurance, counting not only our lives dear unto us, but even our temporal ease and comfort. "We have sought to please ourselves," instead of "pleasing every one his neighbor, for his good to edification." We have not "borne one another's burdens; so fulfilling the law of Christ." We have been worldly and covetous. We have not presented ourselves unto God as "living sacrifices," laying ourselves, our lives, our substance, our time, our strength, our faculties—our all—upon His altar. We seem altogether to have lost sight of this self-sacrificing principle on which even as Christians, but much more as ministers, we are called upon to act. We have had little idea of anything

like *sacrifice* at all. Up to the point where a sacrifice was demanded, we may have been willing to go, but there we stood; counting it unnecessary, perhaps calling it imprudent and unadvised, to proceed further. Yet ought not the life of every Christian, especially of every minister, to be a life of self-sacrifice and self-denial throughout, even as was the life of Him who "pleased not himself"?

4. *We have been slothful.* We have been sparing of our toil. We have not endured hardness as good soldiers of Jesus Christ. Even when we have been instant *in* season, we have not been so *out* of season; neither have we sought to gather up the fragments of our time, that not a moment might be thrown idly or unprofitably away. Precious hours and days have been wasted in sloth, in company, in pleasure, in idle or desultory reading, that might have been devoted to the closet, the study, the pulpit or the meeting! Indolence, self-indulgence, fickleness, flesh-pleasing, have eaten like a canker into our ministry, arresting the blessing and marring our success.

It can not be said of us, "For my name's sake thou hast labored, and hast not fainted." Alas! we have fainted, or at least grown "weary in well-doing." We have not made conscience of our work. We have not dealt honestly with the church to which we pledged the vows of ordination. We have dealt deceitfully with God, whose servants we profess to be. We have manifested but little of the unwearied, self-denying love with which, as shepherds, we ought to have watched over the flocks committed to our care. We have fed ourselves, and not the flock.*

---

* Hear Richard Baxter's statement of his usual ministerial duties, in answer to some enemies who taunted him with idleness: "The worst I wish you is that you had my ease instead of your labor. I have reason to take myself for the least of all saints, and yet I fear not to tell the accuser that I take labor of most tradesmen in the town to be a pleasure to the body in comparison with mine, though I would not exchange it with the greatest prince. Their labor preserveth health, and mine consumeth it; they work in ease, and I in continual pain; they have hours and days of recreation, I have scarce time to eat and drink. Nobody molesteth them for their labor, but the more I do, the more hatred and trouble I draw upon me." This is "spending and being spent"; this is an example worthy of imitation.

5. *We have been cold.* Even when diligent, how little warmth and glow! The whole soul is not poured into the duty, and hence it wears too often the repulsive air of routine and form. We do not speak and act like men in earnest. Our words are feeble, even when sound and true; our looks are careless, even when our words are weighty; and our tones betray the apathy which both words and looks disguise. Love is wanting, deep love, love strong as death, love such as made Jeremiah weep in secret places for the pride of Israel, and Paul speak "even weeping" of the enemies of the cross of Christ. In preaching and visiting, in counseling and reproving, what formality, what coldness, how little tenderness and affection! "Oh that I was all heart," said Rowland Hill, "and soul, and spirit, to tell the glorious gospel of Christ to perishing multitudes!"

Afraid to Tell the Whole Truth

6. *We have been timid.* Fear has often led us to smooth down or generalize truths which if broadly stated must have brought hatred and reproach upon us. We have thus often failed to declare to our people the whole counsel of God. We have shrunk from reproving, rebuking and exhorting with all long-suffering and doctrine. We have feared to alienate friends, or to awaken the wrath of enemies. Hence our preaching of the law has been feeble and straitened; and hence our preaching of a free gospel has been yet more vague, uncertain and timorous. We are greatly deficient in that majestic boldness and nobility of spirit which peculiarly marked Luther, Calvin, Knox, and the mighty men of the Reformation. Of Luther it was said, "every word was a thunderbolt."

7. *We have been wanting in solemnity.* In reading the lives of Howe or Baxter, of Brainerd or Edwards, we are in company with men who in solemnity of deportment and gravity of demeanor were truly of the apostolic school. We feel that these men must have carried weight with them, both in their words

and lives. We see also the contrast between ourselves and them in respect of that deep solemnity of air and tone which made men feel that they walked with God. How deeply ought we to be abased at our levity, frivolity, flippancy, vain mirth, foolish talking and jesting, by which grievous injury has been done to souls, the progress of the saints retarded, and the world countenanced in its wretched vanities.

Preaching Self Instead of Christ

8. *We have preached ourselves, not Christ.* We have sought applause, courted honor, been avaricious of fame and jealous of our reputation. We have preached too often so as to exalt ourselves instead of magnifying Christ, so as to draw men's eyes to ourselves instead of fixing them on Him and His cross. Nay, and have we not often preached Christ for the very purpose of getting honor to ourselves? Christ, in the sufferings of His first coming and the glory of His second, has not been the Alpha and Omega, the first and the last, of all our sermons.

9. *We have used words of man's wisdom.* We have forgotten Paul's resolution to avoid the enticing words of man's wisdom, lest he should make the cross of Christ of none effect. We have reversed his reasoning as well as his resolution, and acted as if by well-studied, well-polished, well-reasoned discourses, we could so gild and beautify the cross as to make it no longer repulsive, but irresistibly attractive to the carnal eye! Hence we have often sent men home well satisfied with themselves, convinced that they were religious because they were affected by our eloquence, touched by our appeals or persuaded by our arguments. In this way we have made the cross of Christ of none effect and sent souls to hell with a lie in their right hand. Thus, by avoiding the offense of the cross and the foolishness of preaching we have had to labor in vain, and mourn over an unblest, unfruitful ministry.

10. *We have not fully preached a free gospel.* We have been

afraid of making it *too free*, lest men should be led into licentiousness; as if it were possible to preach too free a gospel, or as if its *freeness* could lead men into sin. It is only a free gospel that can bring peace, and it is only a free gospel that can make men holy. Luther's preaching was summed up in these two points—"that we are justified by faith alone, and that we must be assured that we are justified"; and it was this that he urged his brother Brentius to preach; and it was by such free, full, bold preaching of the glorious gospel, untrammeled by works, merits, terms, conditions, and unclouded by the fancied humility of doubts, fears, uncertainties, that such blessed success accompanied his labors. Let us go and do likewise. Allied to this is the necessity of insisting on the sinner's *immediate* turning to God, and demanding in the Master's name the sinner's *immediate* surrender of heart to Christ. Strange that sudden conversions should be so much disliked by some ministers. They are the most scriptural of all conversions.

Too Little Emphasis on God's Word

11. *We have not duly studied and honored the Word of God.* We have given a greater prominence to man's writings, man's opinions, man's systems in our studies than to the WORD. We have drunk more out of human cisterns than divine. We have held more communion with man than God. Hence the mold and fashion of our spirits, our lives, our words, have been derived more from man than God. We must study the Bible more. We must steep our souls in it. We must not only lay it up within us, but transfuse it through the whole texture of the soul.

12. *We have not been men of prayer.* The spirit of prayer has slumbered amongst us. The closet has been too little frequented and delighted in. We have allowed business, study or active labor to interfere with our closet-hours. And the feverish atmosphere in which both the church and nation are enveloped

has found its way into our closet, disturbing the sweet calm of its blessed solitude. Sleep, company, idle visiting, foolish talking and jesting, idle reading, unprofitable occupations, engross time that might have been redeemed for prayer.

Time for Everything but Prayer

Why is there so little anxiety to get time to pray? Why is there so little forethought in the laying out of time and employments so as to secure a large portion of each day for prayer? Why is there so much speaking, yet so little prayer? Why is there so much running to and fro, yet so little prayer? Why so much bustle and business, yet so little prayer? Why so many meetings with our fellow-men, yet so few meetings with God? Why so little being alone, so little thirsting of the soul for the calm, sweet hours of unbroken solitude, when God and His child hold fellowship together as if they could never part? It is the want of these solitary hours that not only injures our own growth in grace but makes us such unprofitable members of the church of Christ, and that renders our lives useless. In order to grow in grace, we must be much *alone*. It is not in society—even Christian society—that the soul grows most rapidly and vigorously. In *one single* quiet hour of prayer it will often make more progress than in days of company with others. It is in the desert that the dew falls freshest and the air is purest. So with the soul. It is when none but God is nigh; when His presence alone, like the desert air in which there is mingled no noxious breath of man, surrounds and pervades the soul; it is then that the eye gets the clearest, simplest view of eternal certainties; it is then that the soul gathers in wondrous refreshment and power and energy.

And so it is also in this way that we become truly useful to others. It is when coming out fresh from communion with God that we go forth to do His work successfully. It is in the closet that we get our vessels so filled with blessing, that, when we come forth, we can not contain it to ourselves but must, as by a blessed necessity, pour it out whithersoever we go. "We have not stood continually upon our watchtower in the daytime, nor have we been set in our ward whole nights." Our life has not been a lying-in-wait for the voice of God. "Speak, Lord, for thy servant heareth," has not been the attitude of our souls, the guiding principle of our lives. Nearness to God, fellowship with God, waiting upon God, resting in God, have been too little the characteristic either of our private or our ministerial walk. Hence our example has been so powerless, our labors so unsuccessful, our sermons so meagre, our whole ministry so fruitless and feeble.

Seeking the Spirit's Strength

13. *We have not honored the Spirit of God.* It may be that in words we have recognized His agency, but we have not kept this continually before our eyes, and the eyes of the people. We have not given Him the glory that is due unto His name. We have not sought His teaching, "His anointing"—the "unction from the Holy One, whereby we know all things." Neither in the study of the Word nor the preaching of it to others have we duly acknowledged His office as the Enlightener of the understanding, the Revealer of the truth, the Testifier and Glorifier of Christ. We have grieved Him by the dishonor done to His person as the third person of the glorious Trinity; and we have grieved Him by the slight put upon His office as the Teacher, the Convincer, the Comforter, the Sanctifier. Hence He has almost departed from us, and left us to reap the fruit of our own perversity and unbelief. Besides, we have grieved Him by our inconsistent walk, by our want of circumspection, by our worldly-mindedness, by our unholiness, by our prayerlessness, by our unfaithfulness, our want of solemnity, by a life and conversation so little in conformity with the character of a disciple or the office of ambassador.

An old Scottish minister thus writes concerning himself: "I find a want of the Spirit—of the power and demonstration of the Spirit—in praying, speaking, and exhorting; that whereby men are mainly convinced, and whereby they are a terror and a wonder unto others, so as they stand in awe of them; that glory and majesty whereby respect and reverence are procured; that whereby Christ's sermons were differenced from those of the Scribes and Pharisees; which I judge to be the beams of God's majesty and of the Spirit of holiness breaking out and shining through His people. But my foul garments are on! Woe is me! the crown of glory and majesty is fallen off my head; my words are weak and carnal, not mighty; whereby contempt is bred. No remedy for this but humility, self-loathing and a striving to maintain fellowship with God."

Too Little Imitation of Christ

14. *We have had little of the mind of Christ.* We have come far short of the example of the apostles, much more of Christ; we are far behind the servants, much farther behind the Master. We have had little of the grace, the compassion, the meekness, the lowliness, the love of God's eternal Son. His weeping over Jerusalem is a feeling in which we have but little heartfelt sympathy. His "seeking of the lost" is little imitated by us. His unwearied "teaching of the multitudes" we shrink from as too much for flesh and blood. His days of fasting, His nights of watchfulness and prayer, are not fully realized as models for us to copy. His counting not His life dear unto Him that He might glorify the Father and finish the work given Him to do, is but little remembered by us as the principle on which we are to act. Yet surely we are to follow His steps; the servant is to walk where his Master has led the way; the under shepherd is to be what the Chief Shepherd was. We must not seek rest or ease in a world where He whom we love had none.

V

REVIVAL IN THE MINISTRY

It is easier to speak or write about revival than to set about it. There is so much rubbish to be swept out, so many self-raised hindrances to be dealt with, so many old habits to be overcome, so much sloth and easy-mindedness to be contended with, so much of ministerial routine to be broken through, and so much crucifixion, both of self and of the world, to be undergone. As Christ said of the unclean spirit which the disciples could not cast out, so we may say of these: "This kind goeth not out but by prayer and fasting."

So thought a minister in the seventeenth century; for, after lamenting the evils both of his life and his ministry, he thus resolves to set about their renewal:

"(1) In imitation of Christ and His apostles, and to get good done, I purpose to rise timely every morning.

"(2) To prepare as soon as I am up some work to be done, and how and when to do it; to engage my heart to it; and at even to call myself to account and to mourn over my failings.

"(3) To spend a sufficient portion of time every day in prayer, reading, meditating, spiritual exercises: morning, mid-day, evening, and ere I go to bed.

"(4) Once in the month, either the end or middle of it, I keep a day of humiliation for the public condition, for the Lord's people and their sad condition, for raising up the work and people of God.

"(5) I spend, besides this, one day for my own private condition, in fighting against spiritual evils and to get my heart more holy, or to get some special exercise accomplished, once in six months.

"(6) I spend once every week four hours over and above my daily portion in private, for some special causes relating either to myself or others.

"(7) To spend some time on Saturday, towards night, for preparation for the Lord's Day.

"(8) To spend six or seven days together, once a year, when most convenient, wholly and only on spiritual accounts."

Today's Need for Revival

Such was the way in which he set about personal and ministerial revival. Let us take an example from him. If he needed it much, we need it more.

In the fifth and sixth centuries, Gildas and Salvian arose to alarm and arouse a careless church and a formal ministry. In the sixteenth, such was the task which devolved on the Reformers. In the seventeenth, Baxter, among others, took a prominent part in stimulating the languid piety and dormant energies of his fellow ministers. In the eighteenth, God raised up some choice and noble men to awaken the church and lead the way to a higher and bolder career of ministerial duty. The present century stands no less in need of some such stimulating influence. We have experienced many symptoms of life, but still the mass is not quickened. We require some new Baxter to arouse us by his voice and his example. It is melancholy to see the amount of ministerial languor and inefficiency that still overspreads our land. How long, O Lord, how long!

The infusion of new life into the ministry ought to be the object of more direct and special effort, as well as of more united and fervent prayer. The prayers of Christians ought to be more largely directed to the students, the preachers, the ministers of the Christian church. It is a *living* ministry that our country needs; and without such a ministry it can not long expect to escape the judgments of God. *We need men that will spend and be spent—that will labor and pray—that will watch and weep for souls.*

How Myconius Learned His Lesson

In the life of Myconius, the friend of Luther, as given by Melchior Adam, we have the following beautiful and striking account of an event which proved the turning point in his history and led him to devote his energies to the cause of Christ. The first night that he entered the monastery, intending to become a monk, he dreamed; and it seemed as if he was ranging a vast wilderness alone. Suddenly a guide appeared and led him onwards to a most lovely vale, watered by a pleasant stream of which he was not permitted to taste, and then to a marble fountain of pure water. He tried to kneel and drink, when, lo! a crucified Saviour stood forth to view, from whose wounds gushed the copious stream. In a moment his guide flung him into the fountain. His mouth met the flowing wounds and he drank most sweetly, never to thirst again!

No sooner was he refreshed himself than he was led away by his guide to be taught what great things he was yet to do for the crucified One whose precious wounds had poured the living water into his soul. He came to a wide stretching plain covered with waving grain. His guide ordered him to reap. He excused himself by saying that he was wholly unskilled in such labor. "What you know not you shall learn," was the reply. They came nearer, and he saw a solitary reaper toiling at the sickle with such prodigious effort as if he were determined to reap the whole field himself. The guide ordered him to join this laborer, and seizing a sickle, showed him how to proceed.

Again, the guide led him to a hill. He surveyed the vast plain beneath him, and, wondering, asked how long it would take to reap such a field with so few laborers. "Before winter the last sickle must be thrust in," replied his guide. "Proceed with all your might. The Lord of the harvest will send more reapers soon." Wearied with his labor, Myconius rested for a little. Again the crucified One was at his side, wasted and marred in form. The guide laid his hand on Myconius, saying: "You must be conformed to Him."

With these words the dreamer awoke. But he awoke to a life of zeal and love. He found the Saviour for his own soul, and he went forth to preach of Him to others. He took his place by the side of that noble reaper, Martin Luther. He was stimulated by his example, and toiled with him in the vast field till laborers arose on every side and the harvest was reaped before the winter came. The lesson to us is, thrust in your sickles. The fields are white, and they are wide in compass; the laborers are few, but there are some devoted ones toiling there already. In other years we have seen Whitefield and Hill putting forth their enormous efforts, as if they would reap the whole field alone. Let us join ourselves to such men, and the Lord of the harvest will not leave us to toil alone.

Reaping the Great Harvest

"When do you intend to stop?" was the question once put by a friend to Rowland Hill. "Not till we have carried all before us," was the prompt reply. Such is our answer too. The fields are vast, the grain whitens, the harvest waves; and through grace we shall go forth with our sickles, never to rest till we shall lie down where the Lamb himself shall lead us, by the living fountains of waters, where God shall wipe off the sweat of toil from our weary foreheads and dry up all the tears of earth from our weeping eyes. Some of us are young and fresh; many days may yet be, in the providence of God, before us. These must be days of strenuous, ceaseless, persevering, and, if God bless us, successful toil. We shall labor till we are worn out and laid to rest.

Vincent, the Non-conformist minister, in his small volume on the great plague and fire in London, entitled "God's Terrible

Voice in the City," gives a description of the manner in which
the faithful ministers who remained amid the danger discharged
their solemn duties to the dying inhabitants, and of the manner
in which the terror-stricken multitudes hung with breathless
eagerness upon their lips, to drink in salvation ere the dreaded
pestilence had swept them away to the tomb. Churches were
flung open, but the pulpits were silent, for there was none to
occupy them; the hirelings had fled.

Preaching to Plague Victims

Then did God's faithful band of persecuted ones come forth
from their hiding-places to fill the forsaken pulpits. Then did
they stand up in the midst of the dying and the dead, to proclaim eternal life to men who were expecting death before the
morrow. They preached in season and out of season. Week-day
or Sunday was the same to them. The hour might be canonical
or uncanonical, it mattered not; they did not stand upon nice
points of ecclesiastical regularity or irregularity; they lifted up
their voices like trumpets, and spared not. Every sermon might
be their last. Graves were lying open around them; life seemed
now not merely a handbreadth but a hairbreadth; death was
nearer now than ever; eternity stood out in all its vast reality;
souls were felt to be precious; opportunities were no longer to
be trifled away; every hour possessed a value beyond the wealth
of kingdoms; the world was now a passing, vanishing shadow,
and man's days on earth had been cut down from threescore
years and ten into the twinkling of an eye!

Oh, how they preached! No polished periods, no learned
arguments, no labored paragraphs, chilled their appeals or ren-
dered their discourses unintelligible. No fear of man, no love of
popular applause, no ever-scrupulous dread of strong expressions, no fear of *excitement* or enthusiasm, prevented them
from pouring out the whole fervor of their hearts, that yearned
with tenderness unutterable over dying souls.

"Old Time," says Vincent, "seemed to stand at the head of
the pulpit with his great scythe, saying with a hoarse voice,
'Work while it is called to-day: at night I will mow thee down.'
Grim Death seemed to stand at the side of the pulpit, with its
sharp arrow, saying, 'Do thou shoot God's arrows, and I will
shoot mine.' The grave seemed to lie open at the foot of the
pulpit, with dust in her bosom, saying—

> 'Louden thy cry
> To God,
> To men,
> And now fulfill thy trust;
> Here thou must lie—
> Mouth stopped,
> Breath gone,
> And silent in the dust.'

"Ministers now had awakening calls to seriousness and fervor in their ministerial work, to preach on the side and brink of
the pit into which thousands were tumbling. There was such a
vast concourse of people in the churches where these ministers
were to be found that they could not many times come near
the pulpit doors for the press, but were forced to climb over
the pews to them; and such a face was seen in the assemblies as
seldom was seen before in London; such eager looks, such open
ears, such greedy attention, as if every word would be eaten
which dropped from the mouths of the ministers."

Should We Ever Be Less Earnest?

Thus did they preach and thus did they hear in those days of
terror and death. Men were in earnest then, both in speaking
and hearing. There was no coldness, no languor, no studied
oratory. Truly they preached as dying men to dying men. But
the question is, *Should it ever be otherwise?* Should there ever
be less fervor in preaching or less eagerness in hearing than
there was then? True, life was a *little* shorter then, but that was
all. Death and its issues are still the same. Eternity is still the

same. The soul is still the same. Only one small element was thrown in then which does not always exist to such an extent; namely, the increased shortness of life. But that was all the difference.

Unbelief Weakens Our Testimony

Why then should our preaching be less fervent, our appeals less affectionate, our importunity less urgent? We are a few steps farther from the shore of eternity; that is all. Time may be a little stronger than it was then, yet only a very little. Its everlasting issues are still as momentous, as unchangeable. Surely it is our *unbelief* that makes the difference! It is unbelief that makes ministers so cold in their preaching, so slothful in visiting, and so remiss in all their sacred duties. It is unbelief that chills the life and straitens the heart. It is unbelief that makes ministers handle eternal realities with such irreverence. It is unbelief that makes them ascend with so light a step "that awful place the pulpit,"* to deal with immortal beings about heaven and hell.

Hear one of Richard Baxter's appeals:—"I have been ready to wonder, when I have heard such weighty things delivered, how people can forbear crying out in the congregation; much more how they can rest till they have gone to their ministers and learned what they should do. Oh, that heaven and hell should work no more upon men! Oh that everlastingness should work no more! Oh, how can you forbear when you are alone to think what it is to be everlastingly in joy or in torment! I wonder that such thoughts do not break your sleep; and that they come not in your mind when you are about your labor! I wonder how you can almost do anything else; how you can have any quiet-

---

* A late minister used to say that he always liked to go from his knees to that awful place—the pulpit. Truly an awful place,—a place where any degree of warmth is excusable, and where coldness is not only unjustifiable, but horrible. "I love those that thunder out the Word," said Whitefield. "The Christian world is in a deep sleep. Nothing but a loud voice can awaken them out of it."

ness in your minds; how you can eat or drink or rest till you have got some ground of everlasting consolations!

"Is that a man or a corpse that is not affected with matters of this importance? that can be readier to sleep than to tremble when he heareth how he must stand at the bar of God? Is that a man or a clod of clay that can rise or lie down without being deeply affected with his everlasting estate? that can follow his worldly business but make nothing of the great business of salvation or damnation; and that, when they know it is hard at hand? Truly, Sirs, when I think of the weight of the matter, I wonder at the very best of God's saints upon earth, that they are no better, and do no more in so weighty a case. I wonder at those whom the world accounteth more holy than necessary, and scorns for making too much ado, that they can put off Christ and their souls with so little; that they pour not out their souls in every supplication; that they are not more taken up with God; that their thoughts are not more serious in preparation of their accounts. I wonder that they be not an hundred times more strict in their lives, and more laborious and unwearied in striving for the crown than they are.

"Ready to Tremble"

"And for myself, as I am ashamed of my dull and careless heart, and of my slow and unprofitable course of life; so, the Lord knows, I am ashamed of every sermon I preach; when I think what I have been speaking of, and who sent me, and that men's salvation or damnation is so much concerned in it, I am ready to tremble lest God should judge me as a slighter of His truths and the souls of men, and lest in the best sermon I should be guilty of their blood. Methinks we should not speak a word to men in matters of such consequence without tears, or the greatest earnestness that possibly we can; were not we too much guilty of the sin which we reprove, it would be so."

We are not in *earnest* either in preaching or in hearing. If we were, could we be so cold, so prayerless, so inconsistent, so slothful, so worldly, so unlike men whose business is all about eternity? We must be more in earnest if we would win souls. We must be more in earnest if we would walk in the footsteps of our beloved Lord, or if we would fulfill the vows that are upon us. We must be more in earnest if we would be less than hypocrites. We must be more in earnest if we would finish our course with joy, and obtain the crown at the Master's coming. We must work while it is day; *the night cometh when no man can work.*

Printed in the United States
108074LV00001B/256/A